...nancially Successful

Vending Business:

With Companion CD-ROM

SODA

D1593571

By Donald Rodrigue with Donna M. Murphy

Middleton Public Library
7425 Hubbard Avenue
Middleton, WI 53562

HOW TO OPEN & OPERATE A FINANCIALLY SUCCESSFUL
VENDING BUSINESS: WITH COMPANION CD-ROM

Copyright © 2011 Atlantic Publishing Group, Inc.
1405 SW 6th Avenue • Ocala, Florida 34471 • Phone 800-814-1132 • Fax 352-622-1875
Web site: www.atlantic-pub.com • E-mail: sales@atlantic-pub.com
SAN Number: 268-1250

Library of Congress Cataloging-in-Publication Data

Murphy, Donna Marie, 1965-
  How to open & operate a financially successful vending business : with companion CD-ROM /
by Donna Marie Murphy.
      p. cm.
  Includes bibliographical references and index.
  ISBN-13: 978-1-60138-278-8 (alk. paper)
  ISBN-10: 1-60138-278-2 (alk. paper)
  1. Vending machines. 2. Vending machines--United States. 3. New business enterprises-
-Management. I. Title. II. Title: How to open and operate a financially successful vending
business.
  HF5483.M87 2010
  658.8'7--dc22
                              2010003299

PROJECT MANAGER: Erin Everhart • PEER REVIEWER: Marilee Griffin • EDITOR: Rebecca Bentz
PRE-PRESS & PRODUCTION DESIGN: Holly Marie Gibbs • INTERIOR DESIGN: Harrison Kuo
FRONT COVER DESIGN: Meg Buchner • meg@megbuchner.com
BACK COVER DESIGN: Jackie Miller • millerjackiej@gmail.com

We recently lost our beloved pet "Bear," who was not only our best and dearest friend but also the "Vice President of Sunshine" here at Atlantic Publishing. He did not receive a salary but worked tirelessly 24 hours a day to please his parents. Bear was a rescue dog that turned around and showered myself, my wife, Sherri, his grand-

parents Jean, Bob, and Nancy, and every person and animal he met (maybe not rabbits) with friendship and love. He made a lot of people smile every day.

We wanted you to know that a portion of the profits of this book will be donated to The Humane Society of the United States. *–Douglas & Sherri Brown*

The human-animal bond is as old as human history. We cherish our animal companions for their unconditional affection and acceptance. We feel a thrill when we glimpse wild creatures in their natural habitat or in our own backyard.

Unfortunately, the human-animal bond has at times been weakened. Humans have exploited some animal species to the point of extinction.

The Humane Society of the United States makes a difference in the lives of animals here at home and worldwide. The HSUS is dedicated to creating a world where our relationship with animals is guided by compassion. We seek a truly humane society in which animals are respected for their intrinsic value, and where the human-animal bond is strong.

Want to help animals? We have plenty of suggestions. Adopt a pet from a local shelter, join The Humane Society and be a part of our work to help companion animals and wildlife. You will be funding our educational, legislative, investigative and outreach projects in the U.S. and across the globe.

Or perhaps you'd like to make a memorial donation in honor of a pet, friend or relative? You can through our Kindred Spirits program. And if you'd like to contribute in a more structured way, our Planned Giving Office has suggestions about estate planning, annuities, and even gifts of stock that avoid capital gains taxes.

Maybe you have land that you would like to preserve as a lasting habitat for wildlife. Our Wildlife Land Trust can help you. Perhaps the land you want to share is a backyard—that's enough. Our Urban Wildlife Sanctuary Program will show you how to create a habitat for your wild neighbors.

So you see, it's easy to help animals. And The HSUS is here to help.

THE HUMANE SOCIETY
OF THE UNITED STATES.

2100 L Street NW • Washington, DC 20037 • 202-452-1100
www.hsus.org

TRADEMARK STATEMENT

TABLE OF CONTENTS

Chapter 8: Servicing Your Machines   127

Chapter 9: Merchandising and Inventory Control 141

Chapter 10: Growing Wisely   163

Chapter 11: Off-road Requirements   187

Chapter 12: Exploring Other Options   217

FOREWORD

Congratulations! You have now taken a step forward to becoming your own business owner.

The perfect vending business is one where life is gentle and the income high. It is one with few complaints and few demands for instant response. It is one where your return on investment is high, where you get maximum dollars out of each machine, where service is easy, and where expansion is unlimited. Both you and your customers are happy when your products are moving fast. New designs and styles of different products are the norm rather than the exception, and you look forward to introducing new items to constantly keep up with these changing times.

Vending is a business that has all of these wonderful characteristics. In *How to Open & Operate a Financially Successful Vending Business*, Donald Rodrigue and Donna Murphy have put together a valuable resource not only for the new vending route owner, but also for the seasoned professional. You took a great first step by purchasing this book to learn some of the inside information and great methods to make your business rewarding and successful.

Just buying vending machines does not equal income-producing power; this comes from putting your machines in the best of locations. A common phrase referred to in the real estate market is also a key factor in your vending business: location, location, location. The more people that pass by your machines, the more opportunities you have to capture their business and increase your profits. Whether you have 10 machines or 1,000 machines, always remember that the better foot traffic locations you have, the better your profit will be.

As a bulk vending route operator and a supplier to other bulk vending route operators for many years, I often tell people who are just starting out in this expanding business to start small and grow your business. Be wary of phone solicitors and vending machine companies who put on seminars making promises or guarantees about income as long as you buy their 50 or 100 (or more) package of machines right now because it is a "one chance only" deal. Remember: You can always add more machines as you secure locations to build up your route. A good start is with some of the "Vending and Business Resources" listed in the end of this book.

With this book, you will also get excellent tips on finding locations yourself. I started my first vending route when I was 15 years old, and I will share with you something an experienced operator told me back then that still holds true today. When you start finding locations for your own business, the hardest location you will ever place will be your very first one. After you acquire your first location, that special sense of satisfaction and overcoming the feeling of "the unknown" makes it much easier to start choosing the locations you want for your business. You can find customers through your network of friends and family or by going door-to-door on local businesses. Simply talk to the decision maker and let him or her know what value you can add to the business with your vending machines. If you work with a charity, also share that information with them. To become more and more successful, you will always want to pursue greater producing locations.

Many operators use locating services. If you decide to do this, be cautious of dependence on locators for the success of your business. Even though a locator can help you get machines placed, many times they place your machines in easy-to-find, low-traffic locations just to get the job done and get paid. Be sure to interview and check references. Keep in mind that businesses close, ownerships change, and things move, merge, and remodel, so you still need to know how to acquire additional or replacement locations yourself.

Being an entrepreneur and running your own business is exciting and can have its ups and downs. This book will guide you through the ins and outs of running your own successful vending business. *How to Open & Operate a Financially Successful Vending Business* includes many helpful chapters, such as marketing strategies, placing machines, locators, charity sponsorships, commissions, and much more. Whether you are thinking of starting with the larger soda and snack machines or the easier start-up of bulk vending machines, this is a great resource book to have.

I found the information contained in this book extremely helpful. Even a seasoned veteran stands to gain by reading this very thoughtful and well-presented guide to vending. You have taken an important first step by reading this book to enter the exciting and rewarding field of vending. Read, talk, and ask questions to make sure that this business is for you.

To all of you who decide that vending is the beginning of a new chapter in your economic growth, I give my best wishes for all your future success in the world.

Jerry Korn, Candymachines.com
Supplier of Bulk Vending Machines and Supplies
Both National and International
More than 40 years of Experience

Jerry Korn is currently on the Board of Directors of Candymachines. com, a leading supplier in bulk vending industry. His first route was 50 machines, which he grew to 200 machines. Vending was his part-time job supporting him through high school and into college. While in college, like so many other people at the time, he was drafted into the service. After serving in the Army, he took his vending business experience and expanded into the retail and importing businesses that eventually led him full circle back into vending. Today, he operates a vending route that keeps him in touch with current trends, while also working with production leaders to help distribute and supply the vending industry.

INTRODUCTION

Whether you are on a coffee break at work, rushing through the airport to catch a flight, or waiting in the customer service area of an automobile shop, you can find a vending machine waiting to dispense treats at your convenience. Vending machines are an integral part of modern-day life. We have grown up surrounded by them. As children, we begged our parents for money for a gumball or plastic toy in a bulk vending machine. As we grew up, we graduated to soft drinks or hot beverages, chips and candy, ice cream, and cigarettes.

Today, there are a large variety of items to buy from vending machines, including hot soup and pizza. Hundreds of these vending items go beyond the food category. You can purchase individual packs of medicine in the nurse's office at school or work; dispense telephone calling cards at the airport or your hotel; rent movies in the supermarket; or purchase pantyhose in the ladies' room. In Japan, vending machines even sell liquor, beer, cell phones, and underwear.

But, vending machines have a much humbler origin. The first recorded use of a vending device dates back to 1st Century Greece. In 215 B.C., the Alexandrian mathematician Hero reportedly invented a coin-operated device to sell holy water in Egyptian temples. It was a crude device that used a pan, counterweights, and levers to open and shut a water valve. After that period, Hero's idea of self-service merchandising seemed to have vanished in the annals of history until more than a dozen centuries later when the first vending machines of modern history sold postcards in the 1880s in England. British bookstore owner Richard Carlisle began selling books in a machine he invented during that same time. Then, in 1888, the Thomas Adams Gum Company began selling Tutti Frutti gum in vending machines on New York City subway platforms.

Within a few short years, vending machines in the United States were selling a variety of items, from cigars to miniature plastic toys to postage stamps. Vending innovations were rampant in the early 1920s. This newfangled craze eventually led to many different types of vending sensations, like William Rowe's commercial cigarette vending machine and a machine that dispensed soft drinks into paper cups. By the 1930s, Americans were taking to the road more and developing a bigger thirst for bottled soft drinks; however, the honor system of selling soda pops in ice chests often found outside hardware and nickel-and-dime stores in need of a technological boost.

Two Kansas City brothers who founded the Vendo Company in 1937 provided that boost. They invented a lid called "The Red Top," a remarkable device that turned the then-common chest coolers into lockable vending machines. The lid was locked on top of a cooler and could be opened after a coin was inserted. Once the bottle was vended, the lid rotated to the next available bottle. This invention eliminated the need to dig through a deep cooler and hassle with bottles that were frequently stuck in the ice. Vendo's Red Top production was diminished during World War II, but the company rebounded during the late 1940s and early 1950s. The brothers returned with several new products, including the first upright soft drink machines that could handle multiple beverages, most of which The Coca-Cola Company owned. The firm also began manufacturing vending machines for coffee and other hot beverages, snack foods, and dairy products, such as milk and ice cream.

In 1956, Vendo merged with one of its primary competitors, the Vendorlator Manufacturing Company, which had been producing vending machines for PepsiCo Inc. and Royal Crown Cola Company The merged companies went public and began to go global, opening up manufacturing operations in Mexico, Canada, and Japan. By the 1960s, Vendo had facilities throughout much of Europe, and the company began producing machines for canned beverages, which enabled vendors to stock and sell even more soft drink products. Now, Vendo produces vending machines for the entire U.S. soft drink industry.

To streamline its business, Vendo sold off its snack machine line during the energy crisis of the 1970s and began concentrating on its cold beverage machines. The company continued to streamline its operations throughout the 1980s and the Japanese corporation Sanden purchased Vendo in 1988. Sanden, a firm that manufactured everything from automobile air conditioning systems to commercial freezers, brought a wave of technological advances to the company and has continued its worldwide expansion throughout the last two decades.

Sanden's new technology included a machine that could stock plastic bottles and receive payment from debit and credit cards. In 2005, the company moved its headquarters from Fresno, California, to Dallas, Texas, and changed its name to Sanden Vendo America Inc. Today, the company manufactures a variety of beverage machines that simplify the process of stocking bottles and cans in the same machine. They also manufacture the Vue 30/40, a clever machine that clearly shows the products and serves soft drinks using a delivery mechanism that retrieves each vended package and places it within a secure delivery port with little or no agitation. This allows for total product control throughout the vend cycle, eliminating products from tipping or shaken soda from spewing onto customers.

As the 21st century continues, the vending industry is changing faster than ever. Companies such as Automated Vending Technologies Inc. are manufacturing computer-based touch screen machines that incorporate magnetic card readers to accept credit cards, use wireless Internet connectivity through cell phones, and have software-enabling remote administrator access. The company's Remote Access Management (RAM) 4000 vending machine features a 22-inch, color, liquid crystal display screen for advertising purposes.

Companies like Sanden Vendo America and Automated Vending Technologies are radically changing the face of the vending world. Vendors can buy or rent machines that accept various payment options or ones limited to debit or credit cards. Many vending operators, who are in the business for the long haul, are now switching to the iVend™ technology — a high-tech, photo-electronic system of infrared beams triggered by the product the customer selects. If, for some reason, the selected item does not trip the sensors, the machine automatically returns the money, forcing the customer to make another selection. Although the user might not get the desired product, the system guarantees more customer satisfaction and less refund requests from location managers.

Today, owners and operators can communicate wirelessly with their vending machines. This technology allows them to know when a product is low or when change has run out, making the life of vendors much easier than in previous decades. By ingesting the information in the following chapters of this book, you can gain a comprehensive understanding of what it takes to start and operate a successful vending business.

CHAPTER 1

Vending: Your Path to Independence

Beginning with the pilgrims on the Mayflower who set out to make a new life in a wild, unsettled land, our culture has valued independence and entrepreneurism. Even so, launching a business from scratch can be a daunting task. The path of least resistance is to limit ourselves to working for an established company or restrict ourselves in a particular career path rather than risk failure. It is less risky if you already have sufficient capital to cover living expenses during business startup. But not everybody has saved up living expenses for three years, which is the average amount of time needed before a new business begins to turn a profit. Leaving a steady job can also mean leaving your insurance coverage behind, which might lead to financial risk in the face of an unexpected illness or accident.

Fortunately, the vending machine business can be an ideal solution for those who cannot afford to give up their insurance or live without a steady income for two to three years. You can easily get your feet wet by buying a few machines at first. This would require only a few extra hours of work a week, enabling you to keep your day job. Many of the industry giants started out this way, gradually building up their machine inventory and routes until they were making enough money to make the leap to independence.

Two of the best ways to get your foot in the door with a minimum investment are the honor system and bulk vending. Honor system vending requires only an initial $15 to $20 investment for the fully stocked snack trays and, as its name indicates, relies on the honor system of payment — where patrons choose a snack and insert payment into a cash box on their honor. Though many prospective vendors are fearful of this type of vending, it can be profitable and easy to manage; a route of about 25 locations would take only a few hours of work each week. It is also the only form of vending that enables operators to earn back their initial investment within the first month and enjoy clear profits afterward. The idea of bulk vending, which consists of a bubble-type rack filled with a variety of loose snacks ranging from chocolate candies to nuts is by far the most profitable sector of vending. Bulk merchandising boasts the highest markup in the industry (200 to 300 percent), with most vendors recouping their original investment within six months. *These vending systems are discussed in detail in Chapter 7.*

Successful Entrepreneurs are Made — Not Born

Perhaps you are sure it is your destiny to be an independent businessperson, and the idea of being a sole proprietor excites you. But before you make the leap from a safe and secure employee to a potentially vulnerable business owner, familiarize yourself with the realities of the entrepreneurial path, and read stories of the now-famous entrepreneurs who took the long and arduous path to success. A handful of these famous entrepreneurs invented devices that have changed the course of history and altered the lifestyle of mankind, but only after countless attempts. If you want to be a successful entrepreneur, you need to learn the secret most of them learned about failure: It is only a permanent attribute if you fail to get up, dust yourself off, and try again.

Abe, Tom, and Donald

The United States' 16th president, Abraham Lincoln, has an extraordinary story. At age 22, Lincoln lost his first steady job because his father wanted the entire family to move. By age 25, Lincoln had already failed at his first entrepreneurial business attempt. He and a partner started a store in Salem, Illinois, and Lincoln was appointed as deputy surveyor and postmaster of New Salem and Sangamon County. Unfortunately, the death of his partner forced Lincoln to prematurely close the business. He lost his first legislative race at 23, followed by five more congressional races by age 47 and an unsuccessful bid for the vice presidency. The only political race he ever won was the presidency at age 52. He also faced personal tragedy during the process, losing his sweetheart at age 26 and having a nervous breakdown at age 27. His unprecedented persistence has become an example to us on how to persevere in the face of obstacles.

Thomas Edison, the inventor of the light bulb filament, is another classic example of a man who fought on in the face of adversity. Some of us might have admitted defeat long before we found out what we were doing wrong. But not Edison; historical records show he tried more than 10,000 times before he was able to get the filament to stay lit and not break the surrounding glass bulb.

Donald Trump, a modern example of success in the face of disappointment, sunk in debt in the late 1980s and early 1990s before finally making his fortune in real estate. His lofty goals led him to renovate the Commodore Hotel into the Grand Hyatt, building the Trump Town in New York City, and several other residential properties. His expansion into the airline industry and casino business increased his mounting debt into something unmanageable. Sifting his way through highly publicized financial problems, bailouts, and personal trials, Trump emerged to a new financial stability by the late 1990s. "The Donald," as he is frequently called, blames most of his failures on losing focus on the original goal he set out to attain.

If there is anything a would-be entrepreneur can learn from these individuals, it is that failure never is — or never was — an option. When Lincoln, Edison, and Trump set out to accomplish something, it was not an option to give up. That should also be your mind-set as you venture out to carve your niche in the world as an entrepreneur.

This is serious business

Eric Normand successfully parlayed his Louisiana-based bulk vending business into an online company, Breaktime Vending Inc. (**http://usedvending.com**), which sells a variety of new and used vending equipment. He said entrepreneurs who hope to succeed in the vending industry must take the business seriously.

"It's not like opening a box off of the shelf," he said. "You've got to know that this is a real business, and you can't treat it like a hobby. If you treat it like a real business, you can succeed. You have got to be serious about it so that it motivates you to work hard and overcome any obstacle."

For an assessment of your readiness to be an entrepreneur, take the following quiz to see how prepared you are.

Are You Entrepreneur Material?

Answer the following questions honestly to assess whether or not you are ready to leave the comfort and security of your present career to become the sole proprietor of your own business.

	TRUe	f alse
Whether I succeed or fail, I am uncomfortable taking risks.		
I do not like bringing work home from the office.		
I am never the first to volunteer for a new responsibility. I prefer to see if anyone else offers first.		
I do not like surprises or the unexpected. I prefer my day to always run smoothly.		
I am constantly low on money and never seem to have enough to pay my bills.		
I get easily frustrated when things do not go my way.		
I prefer to try something new if I do not succeed at something after the third or fourth try.		
I do not like to think about work when I am on vacation or enjoying a holiday.		
I get easily angered with others when they behave or respond irrationally.		
I am not mechanically inclined and prefer to pay others to do small repair jobs.		

If you answered "true" to more than half of the statements, you are probably not ready to be an entrepreneur.

Minimizing your risk

So, you are ready to buy a few honor system trays and two to three vending machines, and you are ready to stock and find a good location for them — but, you have not researched the industry, yet. Well, you have already put the cart before the horse, and you are ripe for a scam. Here are two indicative signs:

1. You do not have your locations firmed up.

2. You have not spied out the land to determine where you will put the machines when you have them.

In any type of vending business, location is the most important factor; the industry scammers know this. They also know that rookies do not have a clue how to find good locations, so they put unreliable ads in newspapers and trade publications that guarantee placement of your machines as part of their package. What their ads do not say is that you will pay up to two-thirds more than necessary for your machines and still have to pay postage to send out their pre-printed query letters to prospective locations. The business opportunity scams are so prevalent in the vending industry that the trade has given it a name: "blue sky vending." *This will be covered in Chapter 3.*

Chris Robertson founded the Toronto Vending Services nine years ago. Robertson started this business with one snack machine, while he still worked as a municipal bus driver. Today he works full-time servicing 35 locations, has written an e-book on his business experience, and gives free advice to budding vending entrepreneurs through online teleconferences. Robertson is adamant about encouraging entrepreneurs to do the homework needed to avoid getting scammed.

"The biggest challenge is making sure that you're starting off on the right foot when you are getting in this business," he said. "After doing your homework and research, you should have the cost factor on the machines. If you jump in too quickly and don't think, you will end up spending thousands of dollars too much."

Finding your own locations should not be a problem if you are willing to do the legwork. You will also need to make some concessions, such as payment of commissions or using charity sponsorships. *This is covered in more detail in Chapter 6.* But first, let us look at why vending is not for everyone, and why it requires more than simply stocking machines and collecting money. If you have trouble getting along with your boss and coworkers, and your communication skills are not the best, perhaps you think owning and operating a vending machine route will be the solution to your problems. After all, your days would be spent counting and sorting merchandise, stocking machines, collecting money, and reordering merchandise, right?

This is only partially right. You would also be contacting your location managers regularly to ensure they are satisfied with your service, calling those in charge of potential new spots for expansion of new machines or replacement of underperforming ones, dealing with customers who have lost their money in your machines, and contacting charities to sponsor your machines. Charles Taylor of Vending Rules (**www.vendingrules.com**), a successful operator who also does telephone counseling to help new vendors navigate the minefield of vending industry fallacies, said there is much more selling involved in vending than blue-sky promoters (those who advertise a big return for part-time or minimal work) reveal to their customers.

"One of the sales pitches used by biz-op and the vending machine companies is that there's no selling," he said. "But that's completely false. There's a lot of selling involved to get your vendors on location. And unfortunately, people don't always find that out until after they have spent a lot of money on vending machines."

The primary problem is the lack of persistence on the part of new operators, Taylor added. These new operators do not come from a sales background and are not used to making a sales presentation. During his telephone counseling, Taylor's role is an accountability partner. "When I first speak to them, they're afraid to just walk up to someone and say, 'Hey, would you like a vending machine?'" he said. "After speaking with me and trying a little harder, they then realize that the third or fourth person will probably be the one to say yes. When they start winning, they start getting enthusiastic about it and start putting more energy into the business."

There is an entire spectrum of under-the-radar customer service behind any successful vending business, which requires a positive image and sufficient face time with location managers. If you are one who has fallen for the idea that no selling is involved since vending machines sell for you, then you have forgotten about the most important item you need to sell: yourself.

If you are not willing to put your best foot forward and convince the people in charge of these locations — no matter how big or small — that you are qualified to provide a quality service to their establishment, you are barking up the wrong business tree. A vending service requires an outgoing personality and someone who believes in his or her abilities. If you believe in yourself enough to launch your own business, you are off to a good start because you can learn good communication skills. The successful salespeople you read about have had to polish their sales pitch in a mirror or try it out on friends or family before taking it out on the road. You have two advantages working for you:

1. There are always businesses that want quality vend-
    ing products available for their workers.

2. Locations are often dissatisfied with the quality and
    service of current vending companies.

You have a chance to prove your company is different. All it takes is that first phone call or handshake. Chris Robertson said his success came from learning to face rejection from location managers, and then learning how to see himself as a problem solver rather than someone trying to make a sale. "You will succeed if you know how to position yourself properly in front of those people," he said. "You just have to be the solution to these people's problems when they're having a problem finding a good vending operator."

Not for the Nine-to-Five Crowd

Before settling on the notion that vending is your ticket to break away from the daily grind of the 40-hour workweek, you have to remove the rose-colored glasses to look closely at the realities of self-employment. People who work for themselves will tell you they rarely get a day off. Entrepreneurs find themselves constantly thinking about the business, planning the next order, figuring out how to make more sales, or determining how to make a route more productive — even while on vacation.

Vacations are a thing of the past

That is, if you can even take a vacation. Bruce Adams, owner of Rainbow Vending Inc. in Denver, Colorado, said owning his own business is fun, but he has not had a real vacation since he founded the company in 1995.

"The longest weekend I've ever had off is a four-day Thanksgiving weekend," he said. "We take every Saturday and Sunday off, but you don't take two weeks off. It's a service business, and when you're by yourself, that's the way it is."

Even while taking time off, it is difficult for a vending operator to take his or her mind off the business. Operators are constantly trying to stock a better-selling product, find a more fruitful location, or even expand into new areas or product lines. There is also the issue of machine maintenance and repair, which is best done during the off-peak hours of early morning or late afternoon. You will definitely be free from the 40-hour workweek schedule, but you should realistically expect to work 60 hours per week instead. After all, the harder you work, the more money you might make.

Sleeping in is not an option

Vendors who cater to the lunch crowd frequently have to wake up hours before dawn to tend to their machines before the noon lunch hour begins. Joe Gilbert, vice president of the south Florida equipment distributor VE South, said anyone interested in starting out in the vending industry should know it is hard work and definitely not a get-rich-quick scheme.

"I've been in the business for 43 years," he said. "I made a really good living, and there are plenty of good, hardworking people in the industry, including the mom-and-pops and large corporations, all of which provide a service to the population. If you think this is an easy job, think about doing it in Florida, where you are dragging 10 cases of soda on a hand truck in the 95-degree heat. It's hard and tedious work, and the profit margins are not that great [starting out]."

After running through your vending route, you will have to restock your warehouse, order new stock, and maybe even pay a few bills before ending for the day. Your brain, however, will not be able to rest, even when your body is. For your business to keep growing, you must constantly be on the lookout for new or better locations for your vending machines. This is the part of the business that requires the most persistence, and those like Chris Robertson of Toronto Vending Services — who was without prior sales experience — could find the task of locating vending machines daunting at first. Robertson had to teach himself how to hear no; he now advises others how to succeed with his downloadable e-book, *Vending Business Tactics* (**www.myvendingsecret.com**).

"I think locations are the biggest challenge for people," he said. "Unless people are calling you, you are out there struggling. That is the most common question I get asked: How do I get them located?"

Chapter Takeaways

Before you invest valuable time, money, or effort into this business, it is wise to know as much about the industry as possible. It is also imperative to assess yourself soberly to see if you are ready for this type of endeavor. Study entrepreneurs from the past and read about current issues and future trends in the industry. All of this information will impact your decisions as you take steps toward becoming a successful vending business entrepreneur.

- Two ways to get your foot in the door with minimum investment: honor system and bulk vending

- No more 40-hour workweeks; expect 60 hours instead

- For optimal business growth, keep looking for new and better locations for your machines

- Failure is only permanent if you refuse to get up, dust yourself off, and try again

- With any type of vending business, location is the most important factor

- Vending is not for everyone

- Running a vending business requires more than just stocking machines and collecting money

- Managing a vending service requires an outgoing personality and someone who believes in his or her abilities

- For the successful entrepreneur, failure never is an option

CHAPTER 2

Business Strategies

You have decided that vending is unquestionably the business for you. Now it is time to begin making important decisions about how to approach your new business. Are you going to go solo, or do you plan to have a partner? What type of business structure is most fitting? Will you form a corporation, or will you do business as a limited partnership? These questions will be answered once you decide whether to work alone, have a business associate, or hire employees.

Going It Alone

The easiest and most common form of business is the sole proprietorship. Once you obtain a business license and complete the necessary paperwork for your specific state, then you are in business. It requires the least amount of paperwork and formalities compared to other business structures, and your income is reported along with your personal tax return. People often run sole proprietorships without even realizing it. If you sell any product out of your home, other than doing so in a garage sale, you are a sole proprietor. If you provide any service out of a home

office, then you also fit the sole proprietor description. Operations of such part-time businesses are frequently conducted without the proper filing of the legal paperwork.

What is in a name?

A sole proprietor can operate a business under his or her full
name or a fictitious business name, also known as a DBA (doing
business as). The DBA is also considered the business trade name.
In the case of a vending company, it will be more advantageous
to create a DBA. This will set you apart from others in the same
industry when introducing yourself to prospective new locations.
Although you could easily name your company Joe Smith's Vending, you will get more name recognition if you come up with a
catchy name for your sector of the industry, such as "Sandwiches
on the Run" for a sandwich vending route, or "Bulk Up Vending"
for a bulk-vending route.

Before deciding on a name for your business, you will want to
make sure it is not already trademarked. One of the easiest ways
to check the availability of a name is to do an Internet search.
Research the name you plan to use to see how many hits you
come up with. But, do not stop here. It is also a wise practice to
check with the federal trademark registry operated by the U.S.
Patent and Trademark Office (**www.uspto.gov**). The last thing
you would want, especially if you are trying to get a new business off the ground, is to face an expensive lawsuit for trademark
infringement. And the names do not even have to be exact. Even
if they sound alike or mean the same thing, your chances are
not good for winning the case, and you would end up having to
change your company's name anyway. When you have settled
on a name, it is important to register it with the U.S. Patent and

Trademark Office. This protects the name from being used by someone else.

The risks

Operating your vending business as a sole proprietorship does pose some potential risks. Because the federal government does not distinguish between you and the company in a sole proprietorship, you — the owner — will be liable if the business is sued or fails to pay its debts. You could literally lose all your possessions if the business fails. A good insurance policy can shield you from frivolous lawsuits; shop around for a comprehensive commercial insurance plan that has personal and product liability coverage.

Although many sole proprietors operate and pay taxes under their social security numbers, it might be a good idea to apply for an employee identification number (EIN) if you ever plan to hire employees or change your business to either a partnership or corporation. Business owners simply file their federal and state income taxes under the EIN just as they would under their social security numbers for their personal taxes. It is also a good idea to check with your state and local taxing authorities to find out if they require a business license for your vending business. You will also need to satisfy any local, state, and federal licensing or regulatory requirements. You could just need a business license, or you might also need a food-handling license. The latter is obtained from either the municipality or county where your machines are placed, or the U.S. Department of Agriculture.

Sole proprietorships operate under a simple income tax system known as pass through taxation. Under this system, the proceeds from the business are not taxed, but rather passed through to the sole proprietor's individual income tax return. The income is reported as wages, and the business owner files a Schedule C — also known as a Profit or Loss From Business — along with his or her Form 1040. A sole proprietorship is the simplest form of business to establish, but it also has the highest liability risk of any of the other business structures.

Bringing Along a Partner

If you have decided to launch or buy your vending business with a partner, you will have several choices, such as general and limited partnerships, limited liability companies (LLCs), and corporations.

Partnerships

Any company with two or more employees is commonly required to register with most city and/or county governments. The fictitious name under which you choose to operate your business will also need to be registered with a county agency. Before you do this, you should also have ensured that the name is not trademarked.

The three forms of partnerships are general, limited, and limited liability partnerships. In a general partnership, all owners are responsible for any business debts or satisfying lawsuits, regardless of which partner originated them. All partners are also bound by contracts and business deals, even if only one of them signed the contract. A limited partnership consists of limited partners and general partners. In this type of partnership, the general partner is the one primarily in control of the daily business operations and responsible for the company's debts. The limited partner is primarily a financial backer who invests money in the business, but has little or no say over business deals and is shielded from personal liability. By law, limited partners must legally stay out of business decisions and operations or a court could find them legally liable for business debts, as well. There are also entities known as limited liability partnerships (LLP) or registered limited liability partnerships (RLLP), which protect all the partners from personal liability. Some states restrict these variations of partnerships to lawyers, accountants, and other professionals particularly susceptible to malpractice claims. In this way, only the partner sued for malpractice will be liable for damages.

Partnerships also pay their federal income taxes through pass-through taxation, which means the only tax paid on the business is via its partners' income tax declarations on Form 1040. Partnerships must also file Form 1065, which is used to keep the government informed of how your business is doing. Those considering a partnership should put each partner's responsibilities, stipulations for dissolving the partnership, and other issues that might arise in writing on a partnership agreement. Without your own partnership agreement, any disputes would automatically be handled under your particular state's Uniform Partnership Act or Revised Uniform Partnership Act.

Limited liability companies

This form of business organization, also known as a LLC, combines the benefits of pass-through taxation of partnerships with the personal protections of a corporation but without having to go through the legal hurdles of forming the latter. Some states, such as California, do not permit the formation of LLCs by licensed professionals, or they require them to go through other formalities.

Although the owners of an LLC are normally not liable for the debts incurred by the company, there are certain exceptions of which you should be aware. These include the provision of personal guarantees by a member or manager to a banking institution to help secure a loan; the failure to pay federal, state, or payroll taxes on time; intentional or careless acts; breach of fiduciary duty, frequently resulting from fraud or other serious criminal behaviors; and not maintaining clear financial, accounting, and funding boundaries between the LLC and its owners or managers.

The owners of limited liability companies can also choose between paying income taxes through the pass-through taxation of proprietorships and partnerships or through having the LLC taxed like a corporation. Although most owners choose an LLC for the benefits of the former, the latter form of taxation is frequently employed when an LLC begins to make enough profit to keep some of it in the business, since a corporation, more often than not, pays taxes at a lower rate than individual taxpayers.

Corporations

Although your initial business structure might not warrant establishing a corporation, it might grow to corporation status at some point in the future. Many larger companies choose this business structure as a way to shield owners and shareholders from personal liability. That protection can also be forfeited if owners are not cautious to refrain from the same types of problems mentioned in the discussion of LLCs.

One of the primary differences between corporations, partnerships, and LLCs is that a corporation pays income tax on any profit earned, in addition to the owners paying their individual income taxes. On the other hand, corporations are allowed to deduct employee salaries, bonuses, and benefits from the bottom line, which results in a lower tax bill. Owners are also free to set salaries, so only a minimal amount of profit remains in the company since profits are taxed on a sliding scale ranging from 15 to 35 percent.

There is also a variation known as the S Corporation, which was the preferred form of corporation for partners who wanted liability protection prior to the invention of LLCs. Owners of an S Corporation pay pass-through taxes as in a sole proprietorship or partnership and no taxes on income from the business itself. They also enjoy protection from personal liability. Forming a corporation also takes longer than the other business structures. Owners must pay a significant filing fee and file articles of incorporation with the secretary of state, or whichever office in your state has jurisdiction.

The following comparison chart will help you visualize the differences in the four basic types of business entities.

Legal entity	Costs involved	Number of owners	Paperwork	Tax implications	Liability issues
Sole Proprietorship	Local fees assessed for registering business; generally between $25 and $100	One	Local licenses and registrations; assumed name registration	Owner is responsible for all personal and business taxes	Owner is personally liable for all financial and legal transactions
Partnership	Local fees assessed for registering business; generally between $25 and $100	Two or more	Partnership agreement	Business income passes through to partners and is taxed at the individual level only	Partners are personally liable for all financial and legal transactions, including those of the other partners
LLC	Filing fees for articles of incorporation; generally between $100 and $800, depending on the state	One or more	Articles of organization; operating agreement	Business income passes through to owners and is taxed at the individual level only	Owners are protected from liability; company carries all liability regarding financial and legal transactions
Corporation	Varies with each state; can range from $100 to $500	One or more; must designate directors and officers	Articles of incorporation to be filed with state; quarterly and annual report requirements; annual meeting reports	Corporation is taxed as a legal entity; income earned from business is taxed at individual level	Owners are protected from liability; company carries all liability regarding financial and legal transactions

Chapter Takeaways

Although this chapter provided a basic discussion of the various business structures, research and learn more about the best one for the business you plan to create and operate. If you are not sure which structure is best, solicit the help of other professionals in the industry or contact your local and state government agency for small business assistance. *Reference the vending and business resources found in Appendix B.* Pay close attention to the business mentoring, business incubators, and business startup advice sections.

- The easiest and most common form of business is the sole proprietorship

- A sole proprietor can operate under his or her full name or a fictitious business name

- For a vending business, it would be more advantageous to create a DBA name

- Check the availability of a business name by doing a simple Internet search

- Check the U.S. Patent and Trademark Office for a more in-depth trade name search

- There are three forms of partnerships: general, limited, and limited liability

- If considering a partnership, put each partner's responsibilities in writing in a partnership agreement

- LLCs can be managed by either their members or managers

CHAPTER 3

To Buy or Not to Buy?

Now that you have decided what kind of business structure is best, it is time to make other key decisions. One of the most crucial ones is whether you will start from scratch or buy an existing vending route. Before you can make an informed decision, it is wise to compare the advantages and drawbacks to each scenario.

Beware of the Blue Sky

Buying an existing route might appear to be the fastest way to get your feet wet in the vending business, but unless you use extreme caution, you could easily be in over your head. It will take a good amount of legwork to weed out the truly established vending routes from the scams promoted by business opportunity professionals. These scams are known in the vending industry as blue sky or biz-ops, and these "established routes" are actually established after they get your money. The amount is three to four times the actual worth of the machines and routes. Plus, the services they offer are sometimes no more than form letters addressed to businesses in your own area. This is something you could have looked up on your own. Another blue-sky approach is to charge you thousands of dollars to send someone to spy out locations for you. Again, this is something you could do on your own for about the same cost of printing business cards or purchasing gasoline.

Charles Taylor said it is easy to be tricked by these promoters. They are experts in twisting the truth to fit their sales pitches, particularly in the amount of money a new vending operator can expect to make. "They say they can't guarantee you how much money you will make, so they will show you the industry statistics," he said. "They essentially put up numbers that don't match the machines they're selling. They're putting up numbers for the types of locations that startups would never get; rather, these are locations that are gotten by full-time vending location management companies."

Biz-op promoters use those numbers to hook all kinds of people, especially retirees who have worked years to build up a nest egg. However, they are not just after those who may be uninformed about the vending industry. Taylor said they also target successful professionals who have cash to burn. "You'd be amazed how many professionals get roped into doing vending thinking they're going to make lots of money doing this," Taylor said. "I can't tell you how many doctors and lawyers that I've bought machines from who realized they're making less than they are in their own professions. They would tell them that the machine would earn $3,000 a year on average, but leave out the point about the time it takes to do this."

The industry is filled with the failures and success stories of those who either gave up after falling for the blue-sky or turned the blue-sky operation into profitable businesses. The rule to remember is this: If it sounds too good to be true, it probably is. All of this is not to say that you cannot find a vendor out there who is ready to retire, ready to change professions, or wants to sell his or her routes. Years of experience and dedication do not come cheap, and an established vending route could cost you up to three or four times its net profit. Unless you are a good negotiator or investing a substantial amount of cold, hard cash, you could spend three or four years paying off the existing routes instead of using that time to make a profit from starting your own route.

Buying an Existing Route

The advantage of buying an existing route is that you do not have to wait for the revenue to grow because you are buying into an existing, money-producing business. You can concentrate, instead, on finding better wholesale prices on your merchandise, slowly stocking the machines with more profitable items, and changing out older machines for newer, larger capacity ones.

Before exchanging any money — and to ensure a smooth transition — you should insist that the vendor you are buying from take you around to every location and introduce you to the managers. In this way, you can begin to form your own relationships with them and see if the locations are as busy or profitable as the vendor says. You can also use the time to note if there is any room for growth or additional machines at the locations for future sales pitches to the managers.

There are a few potential snags in buying existing routes, and these should always be taken into consideration when evaluating the purchase price. Any change in ownership of a business opens the door to personality differences. It is possible you could lose one or two locations after the purchase, and you should expect this as a side effect of the business. This is why you need to put your best foot forward as soon as you take over a route. You can do this by offering a perk to the location manager and his or her office staff, in the form of free soft drinks, snacks, or even a pizza party to show your gratitude. These simple acts of goodwill can go a long way toward cementing a long and prosperous relationship. The same generous gestures can be used after winning new locations on your own to add to your routes. Charles Taylor said the worst thing a new vending operator can do is remain anonymous, as many biz-op promoters suggest. The best way to win locations and keep them is by making yourself visible and easily accessible on a regular basis. "It's all about building a relationship with the location," he said.

CASE STUDY: OPTING OUT OF A BLUE-SKY

Breaktime Vending Inc.
Eric Normand, president
60 Long Lake
Carriere, MS 39426
www.UsedVending.com
Phone: 601-749-8424
Fax: 601-749-8425

Eric Normand is the owner of a successful online vending machine business that sells a variety of systems, including new and used vending machines, hot dog carts, and concession trailers. He first saw the need for a reputable vending business after he almost got scammed by a biz-op scheme when launching his bulk-vending company in southern Louisiana. However, before he signed on the dotted line, a little research revealed just how deceptive the company was.

"When I got started, I came real close to jumping in with one particular biz-op company," he said. "I found out they were lying on several things. They told me they were the manufacturer, and they were not. Then I actually found out who the manufacturer was, and after talking to them I realized I was about to pay way too much for the machines."

Instead of buying overpriced vendors and falling for the company's promise of guaranteed locations, Normand bought his bulk vendors directly from a manufacturer and found his own locations. Within a year or two, he also began buying and selling used vending machines, many from people who, unlike himself, had swallowed the blue-sky bait.

"The huge majority of people who buy into biz-op programs believe they are going to make much more money than they are," he said. "As a consequence, most of them end up getting frustrated and failing. And then the easiest way for them to get over all the grief and emotional feelings is just to get out of it. In most cases, they get only about 25 to 30 percent of what they originally paid for their machines." In 1999, Normand created a Web site for his vending equipment business with the mission of saving more people from the same fate to which he almost fell victim. "We decided to take it online in 1999 to see if we could reach more people like me, who were about to buy from the biz-op companies and lose a fortune."

He eventually sold his own vending route to completely dedicate himself to the equipment end of the industry. Since then, he realized people from all social and economic strata have fallen prey to biz-op promoters. "There were people from all walks of life: attorneys, tax accountants, and financial planners," he said. "I even talked to people from government agencies who had fallen for that kind of stuff. You think, 'If they are tricking these people, I can understand how they're tricking everybody else.'"

One of the biggest tricks they play, Normand explained, is by using the promise of providing guaranteed locations for the vendors you purchase. These blue-sky operators contract outside companies to do the locating, which in turn contract outside personnel to find the locations. Since these people are working on a flat rate, they usually try to obtain the locations in the shortest amount of time.

"They are very few locators out there doing a good job," he said. "They just go door-to-door and find anybody who will say yes, no matter if they have one or 100 employees. Once they're gone, you're basically out of luck. The company you bought from tells you they can't do anything — that it's the responsibility of the locating company."

Blazing Your Own Vending Trail

Most experienced vendors will tell you it is better to start slowly from scratch with just a few machines than it is to buy a lot and end up with them in your garage because you have not found suitable locations. You also need to try and limit your locations and service area to within 30 to 60 miles of your home — gasoline could easily be your largest expense, other than your machines and merchandise.

Before you think about buying machines, study the vending possibilities within a reasonable radius of your home. Of course, this will depend on the kind of vending and what type of machines you plan to use. If you are going with bulk vending machines you will want to check out local possibilities such as automotive shops, medical waiting rooms, large and small supermarkets, hair salons, barber shops, and bus or transit stations. In other words, just about anywhere people are expected to wait. For honor systems, you will want to locate small companies in your area that have 20 or fewer employees and a break or lunch room that is not accessible by the public. For full-line vending, you should concentrate on businesses having more than 20 employees with break areas that are also open to the public.

If you have limited funds when placing your first machines, fill them only half full at first and empty the money when the machine is one-third full. That way you can use the money to buy new stock for refilling them. You should never allow your machines to drop below one-third capacity or your sales will be affected. When full, some machines only require servicing every three or four weeks, while machines in busier spots — like beverage machines at a community pool — could need servicing more than once a week. One of your best investments while learning the ropes will be a small notebook. This is where you can jot down important details, such as the hottest and slowest sellers and week-to-week differences.

Finding Your Vendors

Any successful business needs a well-dressed and charismatic sales force. The only difference in the vending industry is that this role is played by your vending machines. For this reason, they must always be clean, attractive, and in good working condition. That does not mean you have to buy the newest or latest machines; older machines could be competing with a snazzier model right next to them.

Older models, such as those made by Dixie-Narco Inc., are known to last forever with the addition of a new front and a paint job. The National Automatic Merchandising Association (NAMA, **www.vending.org**) has a wealth of vending business information on its Web site and in its publications. Prospective operators should consult NAMA to learn more about brands and durability of various vending machines. You can also check industry publications, such as *Automatic Merchandiser* or *Vending Times*. Another approach is to connect with operators outside of your area who, more often than not, will be happy to share their vendor experiences with you. Since machines will be your biggest investment, you want to make sure you get the best vend for your buck. *For a brief list of online companies selling vendors, see Appendix B.*

A good used beverage machine, for example, can cost half of what a new one would, so you could begin to recoup your investment even sooner. Yet, you should have at least a working knowledge of tools and machinery — or, at least already have a good repairman on your speed dial — if you intend to purchase an older machine, since you might be doing without the owner's manuals and technical support of newer machines. You might also want to make like Bruce Adams of Rainbow Vending Inc. and take a vending machine repair course on your own. He now does all his own repair work and repairs machines for other area operators, which has turned into an additional revenue stream for his company.

Although many older, established vending companies recommend buying new versus old, there are situations in which a good used vending machine would work just as well. Good examples include a snack vendor in a busy laundry room or a beverage machine near an apartment swimming pool. For large companies with more than 300 employees, high-tech businesses, or university campuses, you will want machines with the latest bells and whistles to grab the attention of the tech-savvy generation. It does not make sense to consider machines without a built-in dollar bill acceptor, since people now expect this feature on vending machines.

Adams said he prefers keeping new machines on his route since they require less upkeep and maintenance. In business for 14 years, Adams said his vending machines incorporate the iVend guaranteed-delivery infrared sensor system, which is a positive vend feature that guarantees product delivery or the customer's money is returned.

Mechanical versus electronic vending

There is a significant difference between mechanical and electronic vending machines. Mechanical vendors, which have been around in some form for decades, do not require electricity, but rather use a coin mechanism to verify correct payment. When the mechanism detects the correct amount of coins, it releases a switch enabling the customer to make a selection. Because mechanical vendors do not require an outlet or use electricity, they can be placed virtually anywhere and are quite popular with location managers. Mechanical machines offer a more economical option for smaller locations, but might eventually require the addition of a mechanical bill changer for customer convenience. They are extremely sturdy and reliable vendors that can be repaired at minimal cost. On the other hand, electronic machines need electricity to run a sophisticated, computer-assisted operating system that includes a device to verify and accept dollar bills for payment. Electronic vending machines also require a more complex repair job if broken.

Many successful vending operators, especially those who have been involved in the industry for a while, say they cannot justify the cost of paying for a new machine when so many good quality used ones are on the market. Charles Taylor said that too much emphasis is placed on the vendors when the location is really what brings in the money. "You can't pay $3,000 for a vending machine," he said. "It may take years to get your money back. My wife and I decided that we could not buy these overpriced machines because they depreciate worse than cars."

Eric Normand of Breaktime Vending Inc. said the reason there are so many good used vendors on the market is because the blue-sky promoters paint a rosy picture of the vending industry and then overcharge for it. Part of Normand's success is derived from the fact that so many new machines are sitting in garages because the prospective vending operators never learned how to effectively find locations for them. Taylor added that he and his wife have found many used machines on the eBay® auction site or **www.craigslist.org**. "Many times, these are being sold by people duped in the biz-op scams," he said. "I find that the machines are typically still in their boxes. And I've got machines instantly at a third of the price they paid for them."

By shopping around and researching different stores and prices, you will find many cost-effective solutions for bulk vendors. To buy discounted bulk-vending machines, it is best to contact the supplier directly by phone or e-mail. Talking to someone personally will go a long way toward getting the best possible price out of them. If you tell enough places exactly what type of machines and how many machines you want, you will eventually come out with a good deal. Watch out for the middlemen who charge higher prices. If possible, try to buy directly from the manufacturers.

Safeguarding your machines

Regardless of whether you buy a new machine or a quality used vendor, the first thing you will want to do is change the locks. New vendors are shipped with what is known as a shipping lock. This uses an especially common key, so you will want to install a more secure lock from the onset. With a used machine, you might never know if anyone else has ever had a key, so your best bet is to get a trustworthy locksmith. You will want to have the locksmith key all your locks with the same key so you will not have to be fiddling through a pocketful of keys searching for the right one. While smaller bulk vendors use a cam lock with a rotating metal latch to secure the cash box, today's larger vending machines use what is known as a T-handle lock. The T-handle lock uses a screw mechanism to maintain the vending door latch. This type of lock is sufficient for most public locations, but in less secure areas, you might want to add a hidden lock for an extra layer of security.

Another way to protect your machines is with warning signs and stickers that say something like, "Money removed from this machine daily," or "Protected by video surveillance." Although these might not be true, these warnings could cause a number of would-be thieves to think twice about vandalizing your vendor. You might also consider installing a tip alarm on machines in less-secure locations. These alarms are designed to go off when a machine is tipped at a pre-specified angle (frequently adjustable from 10 to 45 degrees) and deactivate when the machine is in an upright position. Powered by either a 9- or 12-volt battery, these alarms are relatively inexpensive and easy to install.

The last-resort security measure is known as a security cage. This is a last resort because it is unattractive and often uninviting. A security cage permits customers to reach through to pay for and receive products, but prohibits access to the area of the door lock and cash box. A relatively unattractive device, the cage enables operators to keep vendors at high-risk locations, such as inter-state rest areas or 24-hour gas stations, operational.

Taylor said some vandalism is inevitable and operators must evaluate the damage and determine if it is a one-time occurrence or something that will be ongoing at a particular location. "If it's an ongoing problem, then I'd pull the machine," he said. "I have had locations where they just kept messing with the machines. I would rather have a machine sit in my garage than sit someplace where it's just getting beat up."

Taylor said relationship building with location employees, secu-rity staff, and vending customers is crucial to the safety of vend-ing machines. "It's all about building a relationship with the loca-tion," he explained. "I will tell the manager somebody is messing with my machine, and then the manager would tell me later he thinks he knows who the person is and will deal with the problem. Often, the employees do not want me to pull the machine and will frequently end up protecting it themselves."

Taylor also blamed some vandalism on the anonymity of vending operators, who commonly go in and out of a location without speaking to others. "People will commit crimes if they think they are anonymous," he said. "So as a vending operator, don't sneak in and out. If you see somebody in the break room, strike up a conversation. Then they'll see that you're a real person with feelings and a family. People won't steal from Chuck or Laurie, but they will steal from the faceless vending guy that comes and goes."

Leased beverage and bottler-serviced machines

New operators want to get into the beverage machine business because the profit markup on soft drinks and other drinks can be as high as 100 percent. Even so, it will take plenty of canned and bottled beverages to recoup the initial $3,000 investment cost for a new beverage machine. That is why new operators need to consider two different options, leasing and bottler-serviced machines, which are handled by your area's major beverage distributors.

Since bottlers are constantly looking to increase market share, many of them offer leasing programs to operators who need a beverage machine for an existing location. For a monthly fee of about $20, bottlers will supply you with a new machine on the condition that you stock it with only products they sell you. Most will even waive part of the rental fee if you buy a minimum number of products — about 10 cases — per month. The bottlers also take care of all repairs and maintenance.

Bottler-serviced machines are a less-profitable option vendors choose for locations that they themselves do not have time to service on their routes. All operators have to do is supply the initial location lead and a site survey. The bottlers then place and service the machines. You receive a monthly or quarterly commission check according to your particular arrangement. *For more information on vending machine distributors and bottling companies' leasing programs, reference Appendix B.*

CASE STUDY: VENDING RUNS IN THE FAMILY

VE South, L.C.
Joe Gilbert, vice president/
                general manager
4800 N.W. 15th Ave., Suite B
Fort Lauderdale, FL 33309
www.vesouth.com
vesouth@gate.net
Phone: 954-491-7300
Toll-free: 888-837-6884
Fax: 954-491-7301

For as long as he can remember, Joe Gilbert's life has revolved around the vending industry. The son of a New York City jukebox operator, by age 3 Gilbert was tagging along to help his dad carry in records and haul out quarters. Since his father also worked as a bar manager and master of ceremonies at a hotel in the Catskill Mountains, Gilbert was introduced to the hotel industry and decided to pursue his college degree in hotel and restaurant management. Destiny had other plans, however. When his father suffered a heart attack shortly after Gilbert graduated from college, he took over the jukebox route and ran it for three years before selling it. In 1964, a cousin who owned a large jukebox distribution company hired him for the parts department. Before long, Gilbert was selling jukeboxes and pinball machines throughout Connecticut. From there, he jumped to National Vendors, now known as Crane Merchandising Systems, and has never looked back.

"My whole career has been working either selling for a manufacturer or an independent distributor," he said.

When Gilbert joined National Vendors in 1970, the industry was rapidly growing and changing to meet the needs of locations serving consumers who were constantly on the move. The company, a vending manufacturer that sells directly to operators, was already manufacturing mechanical cigarette and candy machines; but, its push to create a system of coordinating, 6-foot-tall vendors soon set the company apart from the pack.

"They started manufacturing a full line of 72-inch-tall, matching banks of equipment, including coffee, soda, snack, cigarette, hot canned food, and other machines," he said. "The competitor was named Vendo, which only made 69-inch machines, and other vendors had shorter machines, so nothing was uniform until National Vendors."

Crane Co. absorbed Crane Merchandising Systems in 1985, and in 1993 assigned Gilbert to a new lower-cost distribution channel known as Glasco. "I was a vice president of distribution for Glasco for all of the United States and South America," he said. "During a three-year period, I went from $0 to $4 million in sales with 30 distributors"

Crane Co. sent Gilbert to south Florida in 1995, but by then he was eager for a new business challenge, and he would not have to wait long. The next year, family members of the founder of Cleveland's highly successful Vendors Exchange International asked him to help start up a new company, VE South. The primary focus of VE South would be on Florida and Latin America. Once again, he put his vending industry expertise to work. "We started with two or three lines of equipment, and I built it up," he said. "Today, we have nine employees and are the largest full-service, full-line vending distributor in Florida. We also sell in the Caribbean and South and Central America."

VE South sells a large variety of new vending equipment and also distributes hospitality coffee systems, water coolers, purifier systems, vending machine parts, and some used equipment. Gilbert said the vending industry has long suffered from credibility issues. This has been due to early operators selling off-brand products, and the image in the media of someone banging on a vendor that failed to vend. Today, he said, the quality of vending products is the same or better than that found in retail stores.

"Now, the major manufacturers are courting the vending operators," he said. "So the quality of the products has drastically improved and the top-name brands are all being offered to the public."

Now 69, Gilbert has served for several years as a board member of the Automatic Merchandising Association of Florida, an organization he said helps vending operators succeed through its various meetings and educational seminars. He advises anyone considering a career in the industry to first do his or her homework so they do not fall prey to the biz-op scammers.

"The first thing they should do is try and contact the National Automatic Merchandising Association (NAMA) and the American Marketing Association Foundation (AMAF)," he said. "Then, they should look for people with brick-and-mortar buildings…and references."

Chapter Takeaways

Learning all you can about the industry and knowing your own strengths and weaknesses will help you make the best decision about buying or not buying an existing business. Be honest about your ability to manage and operate this business. This sober approach will allow you to make clear decisions and define tangible short- and long-term goals for your business, thus minimizing your risk of falling for blue-sky scams.

- One of the most crucial decisions you will make is whether to start from scratch or buy an existing route

- Beware of common business scams called blue-sky or biz-ops

- The worst thing a new vending operator can do is remain anonymous

- The best way to win locations and keep them is to make yourself regularly visible and easily accessible

- Limit your locations and service area to within 30 to 60 miles of your home

- Since machines will be your biggest investment, make sure to get the best vendor for your buck

- There is a significant difference between mechanical and electronic vending machines

- The first thing you want to do when you acquire your machines is change the locks

- If you are interested in the beverage machine business, consider leased and bottler-serviced machines

CHAPTER 4

First Things First

Before you can buy a machine or find a location, you must sit down and determine exactly what your business goals will be. Not only does a business plan help you to clarify your ideas and establish a plan of action, but it also challenges you to answer and solidify questions about your business, such as:

- What exactly will you be selling?

- What is your background?

- What qualifies you to run this business?

- Who are your prospective customers?

- Where can these customers be found?

- How do you plan to promote your business?

- How much money is needed to start up?

- How will this money be allocated?

- What do you expect to be the projected return on the investment one, three, and five years from now?

Working through questions like these will help create a blueprint for yourself, your business, and your potential funding sources. A well-thought-out business plan shows a lending institution that you have put a substantial amount of time and energy into considering every aspect of the business. The more information you have already defined in your plan, the better your chances of getting funding from a lender. Have the complete picture ready and not only will you present a good case to the financial institution, but you will have laid a solid foundation for tracking, managing, and growing your business.

Another important reason to develop a business plan is for yourself and anyone else who may work with you in this venture. It will serve as a dynamic document that can help you keep track of your progress and identify potential areas of growth. Looking at your business plan on a regular basis can help you determine in which areas there is room for expansion, if a new profit center can be added, or if you need to pull back and streamline in other areas. All of these exercises, which are involved in creating and maintaining an effective business plan, can lead to the practice of improving your bottom line by making strategic shifts and changes in your plan.

Every successful business has a business plan built around a mission statement. Get your pen and notebook ready because you are about to discover the basic principles of writing a business plan, beginning with a mission statement.

What is Your Mission?

Are you aiming to be the Number 2 bulk-vendor operator in your city within three years? Do you plan to be the top honor system operator in five years? Will you start small in bulk vending and end up as a full-line operator in 10 years? Whatever your short- and long-term strategic goals are, they need to be defined and refined to a few short sentences as part of your company's mission statement. If you are going into vending as a sole proprietor, you might wonder why you should bother with writing a mission statement or producing a business plan. The truth is, unless you plan on staying a small part-time operation, you will probably want your business to grow. The real value in creating a business plan, even as a startup venture, lies in the process of researching and thinking through your business in a systematic way. Planning your business helps you learn the facts about the industry, consider things you might not have considered a few years down the road, and critically evaluate your ideas to put them in the perspective of a real business. Proper business growth requires a plan to keep it focused and on track.

Crafting a business plan

A business plan is particularly important if you are starting up operations or buying a vending business as a partnership. Clearly defined business goals will help steer your company away from costly side ventures that detract from the company's primary focus. You will also find that one of the first things prospective investors will ask to see when evaluating your company is the business plan. They are a lot more willing to invest in a company that has a clearly defined purpose and growth strategy. Banks and other financial institutions will also take your business more seriously when they see you have gone through the effort of writing a business plan. Every complete business plan starts with a mission statement, which can be as short as one sentence or as long as a few paragraphs. However, it must convey a few basic principles about your company:

- Why it exists
- Who it serves
- Where it operates
- What it sells
- What benefits customers receive from it
- What sets your company apart from the competition

If you are going into business with partners, you should all put your heads together to come up with solid answers to these questions. If you are going it alone, still seek an objective viewpoint or outside opinion from either a spouse or coworker to help you clarify your company's goals. The Internet is a good resource for mission statement and business plan ideas, with some sites even offering help with writing your mission statement. You can examine sample business plans at Bplans.com (**www.bplans. com**), in the start-up section of Inc.com (**www.inc.com**), and through the Small Business Administration's Web site at **www. sba.gov**. *You will find a sample business plan in Appendix A and on the companion CD-ROM.*

CASE STUDY: BUSINESS PLAN BASICS

Rainbow Vending Inc.
Bruce Adams, owner
www.denvervendingmachines.com
Phone: 303-919-4913

Before the owner of Denver-based Rainbow Vending Inc. even thought about starting up his vending business 14 years ago, Bruce Adams researched business plans so he could write the best possible plan for his company. After he finished, he gave it to several people he respected and asked for their comments and input before revising it.

Since that time, Rainbow Vending has grown from just a couple of machines to include 20 locations using Adams' snack and cold drink vendors and office coffee service, servicing and repairing other companies' refrigeration units and vendors, selling new and used equipment, and buying and selling vending locations. Throughout the years, Adams has gone back to his business plan, which he views as a living document that must be tweaked from time to time so his company can grow properly and successfully.

"You need to review it at least once or twice a year to see where you've gone and why you didn't meet expectations," he said. "It's served me better than the profit and loss statement." Adams and his wife run the company together, with her handling the paperwork and him "doing the rest," including all of his own vendor repairs. He said one secret he has learned over the years was to never have a single location that was larger than a double-digit percentage of his company's gross sales.

"They own your soul," he said. "They will run your company instead of you running the company."

One of the biggest challenges he sees facing the vending industry today is the number of unprecedented company downsizings, which could easily take an unsuspecting vending operator off guard and result in the immediate loss of a productive location.

"The biggest challenge is just planning ahead and keeping your ear to the ground if you're going to lose an account because they're going out of business or downsizing," he said. "One company I had downsized from 300 employees to 60."

Adams also said that for a vending business to be financially successful, he recommends the company's locations be no further than five to eight minutes apart, due to the increasingly expensive cost of fuel.

"I have never sold a candy bar or a pop driving down the road at 50 miles an hour," he said.

Writing Your Game Plan

The business plan you write should be tailored to your specific company and its needs, with room to expand and add sections as the business grows. Even so, the plan should include several standard sections, starting with a cover page and table of contents. *A sample business plan is included in Appendix A for your reference.*

Cover page

Similar to putting on your best suit for a job interview, the cover page of your business plan introduces your company to the world. As a result, you will want to be creative with fonts and sizes to attract attention to the company name, but without overdoing it or being too playful. The cover page should include the company name followed by "Business Plan" (e.g.: Snack Break Vending Business Plan); the business owner(s), which will include your name (followed by sole proprietor, if you are working alone) and the names of any partners or business associates; the business office with mailing address, city, and state; and pertinent contact information, such as telephone number, fax number, Web site address, and e-mail address.

Table of contents

This section will contain the names of each section with the corresponding page number. Individual subsections within a particular section will also be listed with page numbers. As obvious as it may appear, the table of contents is often left out of some business plans — do not make this mistake. The table of contents serves the important purpose of helping your readers navigate their way through your business plan. For example, if a lending institution is reading your business plan, the financial section may be of the utmost importance to them over the other sections. Instead of flipping through each page of the business plan, a table of contents can help point the reader directly to the information.

Executive summary

Although the executive summary is the first and most important section of a business plan, it is best to write it after you have completed the other sections. The executive summary is where you grab, and hopefully keep, the reader's attention; potential investors will likely read no further if you fail at this part. The section should be no more than a page or two long — the shorter, the better. Here, you will describe the focus of your business (full-line vending, for example), its legal structure (sole proprietorship, partnership), your plans and objectives, how you will secure locations, your marketing strategy (how you will win new locations, such as cold calling or e-mail campaigns) and potential future expansion (possibly growing from a sole proprietorship into an LLC). If you are seeking investment or borrowed operating capital, this is where you state how much you need, how long you will need to repay it, and how much of your own money you plan to invest.

Business overview

This section will go into more detail about what your products will be, what kind of machines you will use (used snack machines, leased beverage machines, and bill changers), who your target market will be, how you will buy your vending products, and where they will be stored (the garage of your home or a rented warehouse). You will also need to explain your personal market analysis and why you think your products will do well in the locations you have targeted.

State of the industry

This is the current analysis of your particular market — vending. You will need to gather information from various sources for the facts and figures of this section, such as *Automatic Merchandiser* magazine (**www.vendingmarketwatch.com**), *Vending Times* trade magazine (**www.vendingtimes.com**), and other resources. Be sure to include future growth rate information, profit potential, return on investment, and bargaining power of suppliers and buyers. Wrap it up by focusing on how your company will be able to cash in on the future expansion of the industry and what new products you think are up-and-coming.

Competitive analysis and market strategies

This is a hard look at whom you will be competing against and how you will market your vending business successfully. Novice vending operators erroneously believe their machines will have little competition since they frequently serve a captive audience. The truth is that vending machines have direct and indirect competitors. Take an honest look at your existing or potential locations and see what choices your future customers actually have. Do the employees or customers have the option of an on-site cafeteria or nearby restaurants? Are there convenience stores within easy walking or driving distance? You should also note whether you will be competing against the bottler's own beverage machines and if other operators are located on the same premises or nearby.

Your market strategy should detail how you can improve the vending offerings and service available in your locations. Study what you see wrong with the current vending situations and explain how you can offer a better product or service to the consumers. You should also emphasize how you plan to obtain new route locations that would edge out competitors. Describe the potential locations for your machines in your area and how you will approach the managers. Will you rely primarily on cold calling, a locating service, direct mail, or e-mail campaigns?

Operations plan

In this section, you need to detail the approach you will take to manage your business operations. Are you working alone or with a partner? If you are a partnership, describe each partner's specific duties and areas of oversight, such as who will be in charge of bank deposits and who will be responsible for ordering stock. Will you service your machines weekly or bimonthly? Specify how you plan to handle broken equipment and where you will take it for repairs. Describe whether or not you plan to keep some backup machines in stock and substantiate the reason for your decision. How will you keep track of inventory? How will you determine which products are selling and which ones are nearing expiration dates? Explain what method of inventory control you plan to use (for example, pen and paper or specialized computer program).

Management

If your business will be a partnership or corporation, briefly describe each of the managers and his or her qualifications and work experience. Since your business is new, potential investors and bankers have no commercial history to review and must rely on that of the managers. You will want to highlight the past business successes of each partner, and particularly your own if you are going into operation as a sole proprietor. Specifically mention any past successful marketing endeavors, since vending operations clearly rely on successful marketing and interpersonal relationship skills.

Company finances

This is where you will highlight your new company's potential profitability to investors and the banking community. If you are seeking financial backing or a bank loan, detail your expenditures and the projected date of profit. This section should make use of income statements, statements of capital, balance sheets, and cash-flow statements, which you can create with the help of a computer program, your accountant, and/or your financial advisor.

The most important part of this section is the pro forma financial statement (a statement showing financial data reflecting the business based on a series of "as ifs"). This pro forma consists of a one-, three-, or even a five-year projected income analysis, cash-flow statement, and balance sheet. This can help to determine the need for future assets and additional financing to keep your business operational. It is reasonable to provide actual figures for the first year of business, but be on the cautious and conservative side since you do not want to be overly aggressive and strain your start-up business. For the third and fifth years of your business, use financial projections. Seek assistance from an accountant so as not to exaggerate the values. These reports list figures for each month of the first year and annual totals for the two following years.

The income analysis will predict expected revenues, cost of merchandise, expenses, and your working capital. The cash-flow statement is commonly listed in a column format showing the amount of projected income, the amount of projected expenses, and either a profit or loss for the time period in question. Each year of this report should have its own balance sheet describing your company's liquid assets, debts, and value of equipment and real estate, if any. If you already own vending machines, list the types and approximate values on your balance sheets. It would also be wise to include a break-even statement, which would detail when you expect to be in the black and how much revenue is needed to bring your business to that point.

Chapter Takeaways

You can tie your business plan together with a summary, though this section is not officially part of most plans. The summary's goal would be to briefly highlight each section as a final pitch to close the sale to your potential financial backers.

- Every successful business has a business plan built around a mission statement

- Proper business growth requires a plan to keep it focused and on track

- Seek an objective viewpoint or outside opinion to help you clarify your company's goals

- Use the Internet as a resource for business plan ideas

- The business plan you write should be tailored to your specific company and its needs

CHAPTER 5

Before You Launch

B efore you can launch a new business, you should take a
hard look at your financial situation and decide what you
can realistically afford. Most small business owners will tell you
the standard break-even point for a new business is three years.
Therefore, you cannot plan to take any money out of the business
for at least the first two to three years. So, do not give up your day
job unless you are ready to move in with your in-laws.

Of course, you might be fortunate enough to have adequate savings to launch your new business and pay your living expenses
for that time period, but most entrepreneurs are not that lucky.
That is the reason many vending operators start small, buying
just a few machines and servicing them at night or on weekends.
Whether you plan to start out small or large, you will have to
decide how to pay for your initial machines and merchandise.

Get Your Financial House in Order

If you plan to get a loan, one of the first steps should be to order
your credit report from the top three credit reporting agencies:

Equifax (**www.equifax.com**), Experian (**www.experian.com**), and TransUnion (**www.transunion.com**). The Fair Credit Reporting Act allows you to request a free credit report from each agency once a year, but they charge a small fee for the actual credit score. When you have this information available, you will have a better idea of your standing in the commercial credit market.

A commercial credit application for a start-up business can be more time-consuming and tedious than a consumer credit application, since the lending institution has no history to evaluate. Instead, they evaluate you, the potential business owner, and look at what you bring to the table, such as your credit report, what kind of debt you currently have, if you have any collateral, what assets you possess, and what kind and how much liability you present for them. For this reason, it is imperative to bring several crucial documents with you to the bank for the interview with the loan officer:

- Business plan because, without a doubt, your lending institution will judge your credibility by the amount of work you have invested in your business plan

- Résumé and those of your partners, if any

- Financial proposal outlining the type of loan needed and for what the funds will be designated

- Terms of repayment to detail how and when you plan to pay back the loan, especially in the event of less-than-expected revenues or sales

- Supporting documents, such as incorporation papers or the partnership agreement, vendor location contracts, or invoices

- Collateral to help you secure the loan, such as proof of home equity or other real estate, vehicle titles, and stocks and bonds certificates

- Pro forma financial statements

If you would like expert advice about your credit proposal and how you might improve on it before meeting with your loan officer, visit the Web site of the Service Corps of Retired Executives (**www.score.org**). This is a group that works under the oversight of the U.S. Small Business Administration (SBA). There, you will find a wealth of information on how to assemble a loan package, write a business plan for a loan, and set up your home office.

Requesting a Loan

If your projected business revenues are $1 million or less, when you meet with your officer and have submitted all the requested information, he or she will have 30 days to let you know the status of your loan request. If you are denied, you will receive either a written explanation of the reasons for denial or a notice telling you that you can request the written explanation. The lending institution will also keep your loan application materials on hand for a year afterward.

Loan applications for businesses with projected revenues of more than $1 million are treated slightly differently. Your loan officer is only required to notify you of his or her decision within a reasonable time period, after which you will have 60 days to request a written explanation if you are denied. Your loan application record will be kept on file for 60 days after the decision, unless you request the reasons for denial or request they be kept on file longer.

If your particular bank denies your loan request, you might not be on your own just yet. Each financial institution has its own peculiar set of loan application standards, so although you might have failed to meet those of the first place you tried, you might still have a chance with another bank or loan company. You can study the reasons listed for your denial and use those to help buttress your credit image and polish up your loan package. There are also several business-funding options apart from banking institutions, according to the SBA. These include finance and mortgage firms, venture capital and small business investment companies, credit unions, pension funds, state and federal agencies, private foundations, and even friends and relatives.

So, how much do you need? This can be a tricky part of the financial process. The amount you need to borrow actually depends on how you plan to conduct business. If you are going to stay with your day job and slowly build up a part-time business, your loan needs will be lighter because you will only need just enough to either purchase the existing route or buy machines.

Machine costs will vary depending on whether you purchase new or used equipment. A new, eight-selection mechanical beverage vendor with a 200-can capacity will set you back slightly more than $1,000. A five-selection, electronic model with built-in bill changer will cost more than $2,200. Other models could easily top $3,000. A 23-selection, mechanical, floor model snack vendor with a 363-item capacity will set you back almost $800, but add an additional $400 if you add the external bill changer. You can find single- and double-headed bulk vendors for $200 or less, and used bulk machines for half price or less. You can get your foot in the vending door for substantially less with the honor snack systems, since machines are not involved and the initial investment for the snack trays is only about $5 each.

As a universal rule of thumb, good used equipment is 60 percent of the new cost, but you can find bargains if you are willing to search and negotiate; start your research online at Web sites such as UsedVending.com (**www.usedvending.com**) or Vending Connection (**www.vendingconnection.com**). Again, take time to do your research. Overanxious operators sometimes get swindled by the convincing sales pitches of the blue-sky scams and unfortunately end up with machines gathering dust in the garage or basement after losing locations.

If the loan fits...

When looking for possible funding sources, you must decide exactly what type of financing fits your unique business situation. There are a variety of options, including:

- Personal loans: When an individual borrows money from a bank or larger institution

- Bank loans: These are given to the borrower, who then repays the loan with interest by a specific date

- Credit cards: A revolving line of credit given to a consumer who can purchase goods and services with that money

- Angel/private investors: A wealthy individual or organization that provides capital for a business start-up

- Grants: An award of financial assistance, usually from a government or nonprofit organization

The primary focus when pursing the loan is deciding whether you can afford the business or not. Starting a business typically involves borrowing money from one or several of the funding sources listed above.

A revolving line of credit might work best if you just need money to buy a few machines and pay it back over a short period of time. Most credit cards offer revolving credit. This means you can borrow up to a certain pre-fixed limit (for example, $15,000). Then, each month, you pay a minimum amount, which includes the principle and interest. Whatever you pay towards the principle reduces the amount borrowed and increases the amount available for borrowing.

Term credit loans are commonly used for larger purchases, such as automobiles or homes. The monthly repayment schedule is fixed for a preset number of years (such as 30 years for a home, and five for a car). The total number of payments will include repayment of the principle and the interest. This will most likely be the best option if your goal is to purchase an existing business, since the cost might be higher than what is regularly offered with a revolving line of credit.

If you have had trouble getting a loan approved, but do have access to credit cards, then you have another potential funding source. Although you could be paying a higher interest rate than a traditional bank loan, using the convenience checks (which are linked to a person's credit card account allowing them to make purchases or perform balance transfers) would provide you with cash to purchase vending machines, stock, and other equipment. Plus, if you have a good repayment record, you might be able to get those checks with a 0 percent interest rate for the first few months, or even up to a year. Most credit card companies charge a minimum fee to process the checks (on average, 3 to 5 percent) with interest accruing from the day of deposit. Some companies will waive the processing fee.

The reason they offer these teaser interest rates is because they know consumers purchase more than they can pay for in the allotted time, therefore incurring much higher rates. If you make wise purchases with these checks and repay the amounts promptly, you could find them to be an excellent source of additional funding for your new company. Make sure to pay at least the minimum amount by the due date. Credit companies are notorious for revoking the special interest rate and imposing a higher rate on the balance if you make a late payment.

Another option is to inquire about vending machine financing through equipment distributors. Some companies offer up to two years to pay for a machine, especially if you have sufficient collateral to offer. Even without the collateral, they might be willing to finance if you prove you have a workable business plan. They might even allow you to forgo a down payment in lieu of making a larger, final payment.

If your desire is to buy an existing company, ask if the seller would be interested in financing part or the entire purchase price. Similar to a mortgage company taking back a second mortgage on home, seller financing is an excellent option for those who lack the full purchase price, but have enough funds to interest the seller.

Leverage the SBA

The Small Business Administration is a valuable resource for business loans. Although it does not actually provide the money, it does help secure and guarantee loans made specifically to small businesses. Banks and other lending institutions offer a number of SBA guaranteed loan programs to assist small businesses:

7(a) Loan Program: This is SBA's primary and most flexible loan program, with financing guaranteed for a variety of general business purposes. It is designed for start-up and existing small businesses and is delivered through commercial lending institutions. The major types of 7(a) loans are: Express Programs, Export Loan Programs, Rural Lender Advantage Program, and Special Purpose Loans Program.

CDC/504 Loan Program: This program provides long-term, fixed-rate financing to acquire fixed assets (such as real estate or equipment) for expansion or modernization. It is designed for small businesses requiring brick-and-mortar financing, and is delivered by CDCs (Certified Development Companies) — private, nonprofit corporations set up to contribute to the economic development of their communities.

Microloan Program: This program provides small (up to $35,000) short-term loans for working capital or the purchase of inventory, supplies, furniture, fixtures, machinery and/or equipment. It is designed for small businesses and not-for-profit child-care centers needing small-scale financing and technical assistance for start-up or expansion, and is delivered through specially designated intermediary lenders (non-profit organizations with experience in lending and technical assistance).

Disaster Assistance Loan Program: This program provides low-interest loans to homeowners, renters, businesses of all sizes and most private non-profit organizations to repair or replace real estate, personal property, machinery and equipment, inventory and business assets that have been damaged or destroyed in a declared disaster.

Protect Your Biggest Assets

Would-be vending operators who have owned their homes for a while might consider accessing their nest egg of built-up equity. Banks and lending institutions now offer favorable rates on home equity loans and only require minimum payments on the interest. Taking this approach will raise your housing costs, and there is always the risk of losing your home if you have trouble making the higher payments. Charles Taylor said the reason he started his Web site (**www.VendingRules.com**) and began offering telephone consultations for new vending business operators was because too many people were falling for biz-op scams and risking their life savings.

"I kept hearing the same horror story over and over again," he said. "People took equity out of their house or good hard-earned money out of a 401(k) plan and bought these overpriced machines — and I really wanted to stop people from doing that."

Eric Normand of Breaktime Vending Inc. said one of his closest friends in the industry succumbed to the blue-sky promoters and mortgaged his house to start a vending business. "He was doing the business and trying to keep it going, but he wasn't able to keep making the payments," Normand said. "He started buying some used vendors from me at about one-fourth of the cost to try and balance out the equation. He still was so far behind on making the note, though, which began causing a strain on his marriage."

If you have to risk losing everything just to start or manage your vending business, it probably is not worth the time and energy to stretch yourself beyond your means. Instead, spend your time and energy protecting your biggest assets, which include more important investments like your home, your family, and your health. When your personal financial situation improves, you would be in a better place to revisit the option of opening your vending business.

How many machines do you need?

The number and size of machines you will need depends on the locations you secure. In general, a location will need to have at least 20 to 30 employees or a mix of employees and outside traffic to justify any type of snack and soda machine combination. Anything less would warrant honor system vending or bulk machines. For smaller locations such as these, you might find tabletop, snack and beverage, or mechanical vendors to be the best choice. Snack vendors offer up to 10 different selections, and drink vendors offer a choice of five beverages. There are also companies that sell compact stackable combo vendors, offering snacks and drinks in one complete and stylish package. Of course, if you win a location with more than 100 employees, you will want to install full-sized machines with bill changers.

Because the name of the game is revenue, try to pair a beverage vendor with a snack vendor as often as possible in your locations. In midsize locations (100 to 200 employees), you might be able to convince the managers to dump the individual bottler machines after you tell them you can mix different brands of soft drinks and snacks in the same machine — offering almost the same products in less space. In locations with more than 200 employees, it would be wise to place two snack vendors and two drink machines. Although you might have some product duplication, the extra capacity will enable you to offer a broader selection at the location. Larger vendors also require less frequent servicing. This, in turn, will cut down on fuel costs, one of your biggest expenses behind the machines themselves.

Chapter Takeaways

Regardless of how you finance your business, the bottom line is that you need to have enough capital. One of the biggest challenges facing entrepreneurs is that they underestimate how much they need and do not finance enough to cover their start-up costs. Now is a good time to start the number crunching and work on clearly identifying your financial needs.

- Before you launch a new business, take a hard look at your financial situation and decide what you can realistically finance

- If you plan to get a loan, one of the first steps should be to order your credit report from the top three credit reporting agencies

- According to the SBA, there are several business-funding options apart from banking institutions: finance and mortgage firms, venture capital and small business investment companies, credit unions, pension funds, state and federal agencies, private foundations, and even friends and relatives

- Instead of losing everything you have worked so hard for, spend your time and energy protecting your biggest assets, which include more important investments like your home, your family, and your health

- The amount you need to borrow depends on how you plan to conduct business

- The number and size of machines you will need depends on the locations you secure

- Because the name of the game is revenue, try to pair a beverage vendor with a snack vendor as often as possible in your locations

CHAPTER 6

Finding Locations

Finding locations for your vendors is the trickiest aspect of the business, especially for those who buy machines from fast-talking biz-op salesmen at trade shows. Since these often come with "guaranteed placement," new operators never learn how to win and keep good locations. Before they can get off to a good start they have already lost locations and have no idea how to find new ones. Eric Normand said finding good locations is the key to the success of any vending business. "Definitely for most people, locating is going to be the most difficult thing," he said. "That's usually what makes or breaks people. If you don't get decent locations, your machines may take four years to pay for themselves; if you get a decent one, it may take less than a year."

In Search of a Good Location

Vendor locating is one of the most important parts of this business, and you will always need to keep an eye out for new or better-producing locations. Be careful thinking this is a one-time deal and that after you locate your vendors, you can ignore this part of your business. No location is guaranteed for life, and even the best location can turn sour through a change of ownership, business downturn, or other economic factors. You should plan to relocate the lowest-performing machines at least every month to increase your bottom line and grow your business.

When locating vendors, there are several common methods you can use to save locating costs. Of course, if you find that you do not like this aspect of vending, you can pay professional location services or telemarketing and direct-mail companies to do the initial contacts for you. You will still have to close the sale with a personal visit, but at least you will already have your foot in the door.

Locating on your own

By far, the most profitable and least expensive way to find locations for your vendors is to do it yourself. The easiest way to get started is to make a list of all the prospective locations for your types of machines in your service area. If you are focusing on bulk or fun-size bulk vending, list all potential locations, such as barbershops, beauty salons, automobile service facilities, laundromats, restaurants, grocery stores, and large medical complexes — almost any type of business that services customers or has a waiting area. For snack, soda, and full-line vending, concentrate on locations such as small to mid-size companies with 50 or more employees, hotels and motels, hospitals, college and university campuses, shopping centers and malls, and airports — just about anywhere people gather. For drink and snack machines, consider large apartment complexes and condominium buildings; place these around the swimming pool and tennis court areas, since the residents would prefer not to drive somewhere else just to get a cold beverage or a quick snack.

If you are unsure about the location's ability to support a full-size vending machine, analyze several criteria to provide an estimate of the number of potential vending customers at the location. You can do this informally on a scratch pad or create a typewritten form that can be reprinted whenever you need to do a location evaluation. In addition to the name of the company or business and its location, you should include the following information:

- Number of employees

- Ratio of male to female employees to determine types of snacks to include

- Hours of operation

- Average length of lunch breaks

- Approximate outside customer traffic, if applicable

- Other dining or snack options (on-site cafeterias, lunch wagons, nearby restaurants, convenience stores)

These figures can be easily obtained by calling the human resources office at the location or by asking some of the employees who frequent the location.

Making a house call

The primary ways to find locations and develop leads for new locations are on-site visits; cold calling, also referred to as telemarketing; and direct-mail campaigns. The first two, in particular, require you get used to hearing the word "no," especially if you have never been in sales before. You can never expect positive results from more than 15 to 25 percent of the locations you visit in person. Even so, out of every 10 locations contacted, you should secure at least one location for your vendors. When making on-site visits you should, when feasible, have the machines with you in the vehicle in case the potential clients show signs of immediate interest. Although that might not be possible with large snack vendors and drink machines, you can easily throw a bulk or fun-size snack machine into the trunk or backseat of your car, just in case. Regardless of whether you can take machines with you when visiting prospective locations, always carry brochures and photos of your machines to show the managers.

When making on-site visits, dress in business casual attire and avoid flashy clothing and jewelry. Whenever possible, try to discover who the manager is beforehand so you can ask for him or her by name upon arrival. Avoid wasting your time making your sales pitch to someone who — no matter how nice they might be — has no authority to accept a vending machine. Bring as many visual props as you can with you, particularly if you are unable to bring the machines themselves. These can include vendor brochures and photos, product images, and charity sponsorship stickers, if you have decided to use them on bulk vendors. It is also a good idea to assess the area while you are heading to the manager's office or your pre-arranged meeting place. Make mental notes of the current vending machine landscape, if any; the current vendors available; and whether or not the machines have bill changers. That way, you will know what advantages or improvements your vending machines can offer over the competition. When face-to-face with the manager, offer to customize the products to employee tastes, such as the addition of healthy snacks and fruit drinks to the lineup.

Cold-calling hints

With the telemarketing approach, the percentage of positive results might be lower, but you will make that up with productivity, since you will not be spending time driving from one location to another. The primary objective in cold calling is to pique interest in a vending machine or new vending operator. Ask permission to stop by on a pre-arranged day to talk about your vending service and perhaps show them your machines.

When conducting a cold call, keep the script near the phone for quick referrals and to ensure that you do not forget any important details. Do your best to speak directly to the person in charge of the location or handling the building's infrastructure. If a receptionist answers the phone, ask him or her to direct you to the person who would be able to make a decision about vending machines. That should save you precious time and get you closer to the right person from the start. If the manager's secretary then takes the call and says that the manager is unavailable, leave a message and make a plan to call back. Many people are simply too busy to return phone calls to people they do not know or were not expecting to hear from.

It would also be advisable to keep a notebook with a list of the companies already contacted, the results from the call, and any other pertinent details. That way, you can easily identify which companies turned you down, which ones are possibilities, and which need to be contacted again. Even rejections you get when telemarketing might not last forever. After all, managers change constantly with other variables, and the company that says "no" today might be interested six months from now.

Spare your ego and try direct mail

Direct mail is perhaps the least ego bruising of these methods, especially for those who have never sold to the public before. By sending out mass mailings of query letters with fliers, brochures, and business cards, you can quickly reach a broader audience in a shorter time than by making personal visits or telemarketing. Receiving a positive response from direct mail takes the harsh edge off an on-site visit, since you know the client is expecting you and is already interested in a vending machine.

A mailing list of prospective locations is the first thing you need to conduct a successful direct-mail campaign. You can either have a professional mailing list company compile these for a fee based on your specifications or you can create your own mailing list. Your personal time constraints will dictate which option you choose. Compiling this list yourself would be more economical. It will require time to jot down the locations and find the mailing addresses. Here are a few helpful pointers for compiling a great mailing list:

1. Create a simple spreadsheet with name, address, e-mail, and phone numbers of your prospects. Doing this first will save you valuable time.

2. Gather business cards from everyone you come in contact with.

3. Ask for referrals from satisfied location managers.

4. Capture information about the companies from which you purchase your products.

5. Visit company Web sites to obtain information about the best person to contact.

6. If you have a Web site for your business, include a customer contact or information request form.

7. Look to your colleagues. Do you know a company that complements your own (a bottling company or a

food packaging company)? If so, see if they would be interested in swapping customer lists.

8. Trade shows, seminars, and workshops are a great place to capture contacts. If you have secured a booth, create a sign-up sheet or address cards that people can fill out while visiting with you.

9. Keep your mailing list clean and up-to-date.

Find out the name of the manager or person in charge of the facilities to ensure your query gets into the right hands. Also, do not overlook the value of your inner circle of family and friends. Your relatives and friends work somewhere and know at least one person. Each of them could provide a lead for your vending company and they could help pave the way for getting you a phone call, visit, or contact information to send a direct-mail package.

To help improve your chances with direct mailings, design a letterhead for your vending company to demonstrate more professionalism to location managers. This can be done rather inexpensively at a print shop or through the use of easy-to-find and easy-to-use computer software. The letter should be written in precise, simple language and describe who you are, what you are offering, and the kind of quality commitment the company can expect from your service. If you plan to use a cash sign-up bonus for machine placement, mention that at the beginning of the letter. It could make the difference between the manager's desk and the wastebasket.

CASE STUDY: IT IS NOT THE MACHINE – IT IS THE LOCATION

Vending Rules
Charles Taylor, owner
www.vendingrules.com

Early in his vending career, Charles Taylor of Vending Rules learned the pivotal role locations play in the success or failure of a business. He picked up three kinetic gumball machines, which were popular in the late 1990s, from a man wanting to get out of the business. Two were already located, and Laurie, his wife and business partner, quickly placed the third in a bowling alley. These huge machines had all the bells and whistles, and the bowling alley proved to be a good location.

"The first month, it did about $350," he said. "Because we placed machines so early in good locations, we thought this was easy, like shooting fish in a barrel." The couple's mistake, however, was deciding to subsequently buy three more at full price. That decision quickly forced them to learn the importance of having and keeping good locations.

"That was when we learned that locations don't last forever," he said. "We never had all six located at the same time. Before we knew it, we were in the vending machine moving business." As the couple's business grew and expanded, they realized the true asset was not the machine, but rather the location.

"You could have the worst machine in the best location and do good," he said. "It wasn't the type of machine that was important; it was the location that was important."

Taylor began to visit entrepreneur blogs to gain insight from other vendors in hopes of improving his chances in the industry. When he realized there were few reputable online resources to help struggling operators, he formed his own blog, which eventually morphed into his current Web site, **www.VendingRules.com**. The name came about because of the couple's experiences.

"My wife and I both knew the industry was good, but there needed to be some rules," he said. "So we established rules for ourselves, and that's where the name came from. I wanted to steer other new operators clear of those biz-op scam artists."

Taylor subsequently wrote four e-books — *Introduction to the Vending Business*, *Honor Box Success Secrets*, *Bulk Vending Success Secrets*, and *The Vending Rules Locating Guide* — because so many people were e-mailing him with the same questions about particular aspects of the industry. Today, in addition to helping his wife run the vending operation, he also offers telephone consultations to help people get back on their vending feet. He said he spends much of his time helping repair the damage done by the biz-ops.

"I frequently hear something like this: 'I just spent $20,000 on machines and three weeks later, I found your Web site,'" Taylor said. "So I try to help them cope."

One of the main problems he sees is that people tend to view vending as being easier than it really is, and they do not understand it has to be treated like any other business. "A lot of times, people run to vending because they think it's a magical business," he said. "If you get a machine on location, it's not a magical ATM machine that you can take out the money and go spend all of it. Vending is a great microcosm for business in general; the same rules still apply."

Preparing Your Location Sales Pitch

Whichever method you choose to find locations, you will need a basic script of your location sales pitch. Have a written copy with you so you can practice delivering the information in a natural, flowing manner. This is particularly helpful if you have never sold anything before; you will want to appear confident and knowledgeable about your vending service.

The script should include pertinent information: your name, the name of your vending business, the kind of vendors you are offering to place (emphasizing the name brands of the products that most people are familiar with), and the fact that they will be placed at no cost to the locations. If you are utilizing placement bonuses, charity sponsorships, or are willing to offer a commission, you should insert that into your script as well, although it is advisable not to mention commissions unless the location manager does so first. Many locations will be satisfied with just the bonus of a weekday pizza party and a round of free soft drinks, along with the convenience of the machines themselves.

Study the following tips to ensure you put your best foot forward when selling your vending services to prospective locations:

- Carefully review potential locations for sufficient employees and/or outside traffic

- Order business cards and brochures (a computer-generated flyer will suffice if funds are limited)

- Take and print quality images of your vending machines

- Obtain the location manager's name and title in advance

- Prepare your telephone sales pitch describing your company and what it offers

- Write a query letter for mass mailings describing your vending business

- Order pre-addressed and pre-stamped mailing response cards, if feasible

- Dress appropriately (business casual) for personal on-site visits

- Check out current vending resources or potential locations for machines while on-site

- Determine beforehand what commissions or other perks you are willing to offer each site

- Note the results from each telephone call, personal visit, or mailing for future reference

Sample location sales pitch

January 1, 20XX

Mr. John D., location manager
Prime Vending Location, Inc.
123 Easy Vending Street
Anywhere, Any State, USA 00000

Dear Mr. Location Manager:

I am the owner of Snack Break Vending, a local vending service that provides snack, drink, and other vendors without cost to locations in need of vending services. We carry a variety of state-of-the-art vendors to meet your every snack or beverage need, most of which come equipped with bill receptors and coin changers. We stock them with the most popular name-brand products and will even attempt to create your company's own personalized product mix, if feasible. We guarantee the freshness of our snacks and have a no-questions/no-hassles refund policy so you will never have to deal with bad product or machinery problems on your own. Snack Break will even provide refund money to a designated company official so no one has to wait.

Can we set up a time at your convenience one day this week so I can come by and explain in more detail just what Snack Break Vending can offer your employees and customers?

I will also be happy to send you more detailed information in the mail.

Thank you for your time.

Sincerely,

Vending Operator

Paying for Location Help

If you feel you do not have what it takes to sell your own vending services to location managers, rely on professional locating services. Most of the blue-sky scam artists use these services to initially place your machines, but they will not divulge that information to you; otherwise, you would use them yourself and save the overhead they add onto the cost. Even if you go directly through a locator yourself, you might have to pay an elevated price for their services because many of them use contract employees to do the locating.

Nevertheless, they do provide a convenient service if you are too busy working a day job or servicing your existing route to spend time searching out good locations. No matter whether you are placing bulk- and fun-size vendors, or cold drink and snack machines, there are industry-standard fees for finding locations. These fees range from approximately $30 for bulk vendors to $150 and up for soda machines. The locating fee will equal one to three months of a machine's gross monthly profit, depending on the locator and the trouble he or she has finding suitable locations.

Try to negotiate a better price with the locator, especially if you are looking to obtain several locations. Since a long-lasting location is more profitable than a short-term one, try to negotiate a smaller fee that includes a lump sum bonus if you are still doing well with that location several months later.

Beware of contract locators

Eric Normand said this is the area in which new entrepreneurs get swindled the most and warns against being too trusting of these contract locators. "Don't send them a money order, and don't pay them cash when they get there," he said. "You will have no recourse at all. At least if you pay with a credit card, you can fight it."

Furthermore, never agree to a location sight that you have not seen. You could discover afterward that your machines are unsuitable (too nice or not nice enough) for a particular location. Even though most locators will not allow you to contact the manager on your own until you agree to accept the location, it is still a good idea to drive past or visit the inside of a location if possible before accepting it.

"I know of one locator who drove this guy around to 30 locations," Normand said. "He already had each manager's business card, and as they walked in to each location, he would wave and say hi to the people as the two were walking around. The next day, the operator filled up his bulk machines and loaded up his trailer to deliver them. When he went into the locations, the managers began to tell him that they had never approved a vending machine. The locator had just gone in to each location and asked for the manager's cards and never even spoke with anybody. But it was too late for the vending operator; the locator was already gone with the operator's money."

Telemarketing or mailing service options

Using a telemarketing or mailing service to find locations can also ease the labor-intensive part of securing a location off your shoulders. With a positive response from your bulk mailing — either a telemarketer's call or reply card — all you need to do is show up with the machine, or at least a reasonable facsimile. Telemarketing and mailing services are the most cost-effective outlets for locating services, but you can still improve the results by assisting the locating company.

To make sure you get the companies or businesses you want to target, provide the locating service with a list of prospective firms rather than letting them search for them. You should also limit their searches to geographical area you have determined to be part of the most easily serviced route. You will find that location fees will be slightly less expensive for sites obtained by telemarketing efforts and direct mail rather than those obtained by on-site visits.

You can also save money by enlisting the help of an individual whom you know is a good salesperson or communicator. Offer them one-third less than you would pay for a professional locator to make personal visits to the businesses. They will be making more than they would if they worked for someone else, and you will be saving money. When you find a particular person or firm that works well for you, plan to stick with them; perhaps offer him or her bonuses for finding excellent locations. Start with vending locator companies, such as Vending Locator (**www.myvendinglocator.com**), Vending Locators Network (**www.vendinglocatorsnetwork.com**), or Vending Placements (**www.vendingplacement.com**).

Charity sponsorships and commissions

Since vendor placement plays a crucial role in the success of a vending company, operators often resort to using charity sponsorships and commissions to cinch the deal. Actually, they have become so commonplace in the industry that many location managers have come to expect them. To ensure that your vending operation is the most profitable it can be, and to get the most out of these business techniques, you need to learn exactly when and where they are necessary. Many vendors use charity sponsorships and offer to pay commissions without first checking out the level of interest or the location's need of a vendor.

Charity sponsorships are common in the bulk vending business, since a 10 to 15 percent gross commission rate on a vendor bringing in only $40 a month would hardly motivate a location manager. Those in charge of the decision-making process do like the idea of the business supporting worthwhile charities, at least as far as the public relations aspect of it goes. Also, the consumers tend to show a preference to machines announcing their contributions to a charity over those that do not. A charity licensing agreement will also cost you less than a standard commission, frequently at a rate of about 5 percent of gross sales or about $2 monthly in a vendor selling $40, on average.

Make your decision on a charity sponsorship based on the particular characteristics of each location. For example, are you shooting for a location in which you will be the only bulk vendor, or will you have competition? If there is competition, do the other vendors use charity sponsorships? The answers to these questions will help you make the right decision. A location manager will be happy to accept his or her first bulk machine on the premises, just because it is a service to employees and customers that will not cost them extra. On the other hand, if you are seeking to place a bulk vendor at a location that already has bulk vendors, you can use your affiliation with the charity to win a positive response to your machine and possibly get a more favorable location because of it. Regardless of whether or not you plan to offer a charity sponsorship to begin with, always carry the charity's brochures and other collateral materials to help you convince a hesitant location manager that a bulk vendor is the right thing for his or her company.

Plan to use commissions on larger snack and cold drink vendors as sparingly as possible. Commissions can severely cut into your bottom line, particularly in underperforming locations. Just as in bulk vending charity affiliations, decide to offer a commission only after carefully studying the vending landscape of the prospective location. Decide if there is enough potential business to justify spending 10 to 30 percent of your gross proceeds. One main reason to offer a commission is because your competitors offer it. If your competition is paying commission to their clients, your clients will probably be expecting it. The best way to deal with commissions is to get it out in the open early. Discuss the prospect's commission expectations when you are evaluating a location.

When you have decided to offer a commission or have been asked about commissions, learn to be an effective negotiator to win the best deal for your vending business. If you are offering to place a new, state-of-the-art vendor on the premises, use that fact as leverage and only offer a 10 percent commission to start. If you succeed in shifting the manager's focus off the commission and onto the benefits of your machine and company, he or she will be less inclined to insist on more than a minimal commission. And if he or she does push for the highest commission level, carefully study the location to determine if it will be worth your hard work for just 70 percent of gross sales. If the projected sales at the location would be $200 or more, you might find it worth the effort; anything less than $100 might not pay for your time and the gasoline spent servicing the machines.

Bruce Adams of Rainbow Vending Inc. advises other operators to stay away from the commission game because it becomes too much of a hassle when location managers try to pit one vending company against another to win larger commissions. It might seem odd, but he said he tries to talk locations out of switching to his company just because they think their present operator is charging too much for the products in the machines. "We try to talk people out of changing companies," he said. "Why should you take an account from somewhere else and then have to raise the prices yourself?" Decide if you will use location contracts for the placement of your vendors. Many operators use them because it offers an added layer of security in case a location changes hands or abruptly closes down completely.

Charles Taylor of Vending Rules said he prefers not to use contracts because he does not want to obligate either himself or the location. He simply tells his location managers the placement is on a 90-day trial and either party can choose to cancel the agreement at that time. "I don't sign a single contract with any of my locations," he said. "The moment I'm not happy with them, I don't want to be locked into them. It's the same way for them; I don't want them to be locked in either."

An at-will contract allows for either party to cancel the agreement with advance notification after the initial 90-day period. As far as contracts go, the simpler, the better; otherwise, it will take your location managers a long time to read through them. A lengthy and complicated contract might cause them to hesitate in signing. If a location manager refuses to sign a contract, protect your vendor investment by making sure the machines are properly identified with signs or labels as the property of your company.

CASE STUDY: BUILDING RELATIONSHIPS WITH LOCATION MANAGERS

Toronto Vending Services
Chris Robertson, owner
www.toronto-vending-services.com
Phone: 905-510-7597

In nine years, Chris Robertson built Toronto Vending Services from a one-machine operation located at his own workplace to approximately 35 full-line vending locations he now services as a full-time sole proprietor. He said the hardest thing for him in the beginning was trying to maintain his confidence in the face of so much rejection.

"The most challenging aspect of it for me was convincing myself it was going to work," he said. "I had so many doors closed in my face that it was very discouraging. Then what happened, I would get a location, and then it would give me the confidence to go out and get another."

He was fortunate that instead of falling for a biz-op promoter, he ended up building a relationship with a local vendor distributor who helped him get his business off on the right foot without going into debt. "He told me to go out and start knocking on doors and talking to people," Robertson said. "He showed me a couple of machines, so I knew in my head what I could offer, and told me to come back when I had my locations."

Robertson also asked his distributor what he would have to pay for a professional locator to help him place his new machines. The answer sent him out pounding the pavement on his own. "He was talking about $600 to $900, and I couldn't justify that," he said.

Over the years, Robertson's locating methods evolved from cold calling to phone book directory advertising, mass mailings, and finally, his company's own Web site. Nowadays, his e-mail inbox is full of location managers looking for vendors because they have seen his Web site or read one of the many online articles he has written on the industry.

"I don't do as much cold calling as before because I learned how to better market and advertise my business property in my local area," he said. "Now, I have them coming to me asking me for information. When I go to their place of business, I'm not a pest, but actually an invited guest and I'm in a better position for negotiating."

Robertson has also learned to be a good negotiator when it comes to commissions, and he believes developing and maintaining a good relationship with each location manager is crucial to such negotiations. From the beginning, he tells the managers that the sales must justify commission payments, and commissions could potentially rise in tandem with sales. All of his commission agreements are first offered on a trial basis to see how each location will produce.

Robertson was forced to rescind a commission agreement at a car dealership that was bringing in $50 or less in sales per week but he said the location manager completely understood after he carefully explained the business logistics to her.

"So, I saved a 10 percent commission by just having a conversation with her and being open and honest about what was going on in the location," he said. "It's a matter of how you position yourself to your prospects and customers and how you present your services."

Because of his longevity in the industry, Robertson soon found himself commenting on Internet blogs and writing online articles. After downloading a free report written by Rob Farnham, a retired vending operator-turned-author now known as My Vending Uncle, Robertson said he saw the potential for combining all of his own notes and articles into an e-book, *Vending Business Tactics*, which is now available on a special Web site (**www.myvendingsecret.com**). He is constantly updating the book, which he calls "a work in progress."

One of his favorite testimonials is from a woman who credits Robertson with saving her and her husband from losing a large amount of money early on. She commented to Robertson, saying, "I didn't even buy your e-book, I just read your free report, and you saved me and my husband $20,000. We were in the final stages of a biz-op."

Robertson said anyone who is willing to do his or her homework before jumping into the business can enjoy the same kind of success that he has. "The biggest challenge is building your business," he said. "What I learned was marketing and advertising. I was the guy working as a bus driver, and I was the guy who quit the job making $50,000 with benefits to run my own business."

Chapter Takeaways

Location is the determining factor between two vending businesses with the same machine that offers the same products and services. The profitability of your business is dictated the most by how well you select a location for your machine. This means you either need to learn the art of locating or hire a results-oriented professional location service.

- Finding a good location is key to the success of any vending business

- The most profitable and least expensive way to find locations for your vendors is to do it yourself

- Develop leads by making personal on-site visits, cold calls, or direct mail campaigns

- If you are uncomfortable locating on your own, seek out help from a professional locating service or tele-marketing or mailing service

- Do not accept a location sight you have not seen

- Do not rule out the people you know as a resource to find new business

- Draft a vending machine contract or some form of agreement, even if you decide not to use it

CHAPTER 7

Choose Your Vending System Wisely

V endors who have been in the industry for at least five years boast a variety of vending machines and product types. However, you might find it easier to focus on one particular sector of vending, such as snack and soda machine combinations or bulk fun-size vendors. To decide exactly what sector of vending might be right for you, you should learn all you can about the type of work involved and the profit potential for each sector. Although we will not touch on every type of product sold by vending machines, we will discuss the most popular forms of vending, which include honor systems, bulk vending, snack and beverage vending, full-line vending, and amusement vending

Vending on the Honor System

When most people first hear about selling products on the honor system, they are cautious and borderline skeptical. But, believe it or not, the honor system works well as a niche sector of vending snacks and cold drinks, and might be the best option for starting out. If you are low on capital, but have plenty of time, it could be the perfect solution because the honor system is the least-expensive way to get your foot in the vending door. It is also a highly feasible vending system for companies or businesses with fewer than 20 employees. Instead of investing in a costly machine, you simply need to purchase prefabricated honor and coin boxes, which can be found for less than $3 through wholesale honor box and snack tray companies like Sheridan Systems (**www.sheridansystems.com**). The honor system is the only sector of vending where it is possible to recoup your initial investment your first month, making your gross profit margins truly "sweet." Honor system vending is the least expensive, but it can also be the most time consuming since you will need to place boxes or trays at more locations and replace snacks on a more regular basis — daily or weekly, depending on how quickly the snacks are consumed.

An honor snack system is simply a cardboard or plastic box with dividers for different types and sizes of snacks and an attached coin or cash box. Patrons simply choose whichever item they desire and insert their payment in the cash box. So, what keeps them from taking the merchandise without paying? What prevents them from taking the cash box? The truth is, there is no way around product theft — also known as shrinkage — when using the honor system of vending. But, if you choose your locations wisely, you can limit your losses to less than 30 percent or, more reasonably, around 10 percent. You can make money even with shrinkage at higher percentages, since the average profit margin for snack trays is about 50 percent.

The best way to limit losses on snack systems is to choose locations that are absolutely closed to the public. In other words, try to place an honor snack system in the break or lunch room or reception area that is only accessible to employees. When you place an honor system where there is public access (supermarkets, hardware stores, or shopping malls), shrinkage numbers will soar. In the general public, people are usually less likely to hold one another accountable than in a smaller office setting, and the boxes are often in low-visibility locations. Employees, on the other hand, will keep an eye on their honor system because they know they have no other snack or drink options on the premises and do not want to lose the one they have.

Because honor systems have lower overhead costs and do not have commissions or charity sponsorships, you can make a reasonable amount of money with companies that have as few as five employees. Taking product shrinkage into account, you can earn an average of 20 percent profit per item sold. For example, even if each of the five employees only buys an item every other day, you could earn an average monthly gross profit of about $15. Now, that might not sound like much, but if you have 30 honor systems in place, the net would be $450 per month. If you have 75 honor systems in good locations, earnings could amount to $1,125 a month. Depending on sales, you would only need to check them about once every two weeks. Just as in any other type of vending, keep honor boxes from dropping below 50 to 60 percent of stock to avoid losing sales. Some higher selling locations might require servicing every week, while others could handle once-a-month service.

Have prices and payment instructions professionally printed on stickers to adhere to your honor boxes, or create a design on a home computer if you have the proper software program, such as Adobe® InDesign or Microsoft® Word. You could also simply write the price on the honor box with a felt-tip marker, with arrows pointing toward the payment box.

Once you begin placing honor snack systems, you might discover the need to add cold drinks. Since many small companies cannot provide the sales to justify the placement of a coin-operated soda machine, they might be willing to let you set up a compact refrigerator in the break room near your snack box. Although it would perhaps take a few months to recoup the refrigerator cost — which can be $50 to $100 at most big-box retailers — you can also make handsome profits on cold drink sales, which might even increase snack sales. Create an attractive sign to adhere to the refrigerator announcing the service and attach a payment box. If space in the break room is tight, place the snack box on top of the refrigerator and use the same coin box for both. To minimize the risk of people walking off with the coin box, see if you can somehow fasten the coin box to the table and add a key-type or combination lock to it. Although not nearly as profitable, some honor system operators add an office coffee service system to the assortment to provide a complete snack and beverage service to their clients.

For placing honor snack and beverage systems, you can contract a telemarketing company to call various locations and find out if they need a vending service. The telemarketing company would then compile a list of possible leads for you. However, you might not find this necessary. Smaller companies are often eager to have snack options on-site, especially when you explain that it will not cost them anything. If your client grows, adds more employees, or opens its doors to the public, it would be best to change to a coin-operated system for more convenience and keep shrinkage rates low. By that time, you will already have the location managed and will simply need to swap out one form of vending for another.

Bulk vending machines offer the highest profit margins in the industry, with 200 to 300 percent markups as the norm. Many first-time operators start out with at least a few bulk vendors in the lineup. After realizing the excellent profit potential, bulk vending often becomes the vending sector of choice.

Gumballs are still a favorite pastime

As one of the most frequently sold products in bulk vendors, gumball can be purchased for 2 cents or less and sold for a quarter. This is more than a 1,000 percent return on the investment — a substantial reason why bulk vendors are so prevalent and many operators consider them a crucial part of their vending mix.

A bulk-vending gumball operation is inexpensive to launch and easy to service. You can find a new, single-head gumball machine for under $50. You will also need a stand, which can cost another $35 or more, depending on the quality and weight. Gumball machines can hold anywhere from 400 to 500 gumballs. You can buy an 850-count bag of gumballs for about $23, which would add another $11.50 to your start-up cost, since you are buying double the amount of gumballs the machine holds. So, for under $100, you can place a full gumball machine at your location, where it will be ready to dispense and turn a profit.

Of course, you will not want to limit your bulk vending to simply gumballs. Most bulk vendors are fully adjustable to sell by weight, so you can stock them with dry-roasted peanuts, pistachios, M&M'S®, Skittles®, and many others. Many operators try to keep product cost down to an average of about 7 cents. You can adjust the vendor to provide more items that cost less (Hot Tamales®, for example), or less of the product that costs more, such as jellybeans. The bulk-vending category can also include stickers, fake tattoos, and small toys enclosed in plastic "eggs." These bulk vendors are ideal in locations where kids frequent, such as roller-skating rinks, malls, grocery stores, or amusement centers.

Vending for High-Traffic Locations

For higher-traffic locations, such as employee break rooms, consider purchasing a two- or three-head bulk vendor. These will vary in price, depending on the type of vendor you choose — multiple individual-head vendors versus a vendor that is divided into separate compartments in a common housing. The former are considered nicer, but cost considerably more — three individual heads cost approximately $200 without a stand — while the latter will run you substantially less, around $100. The style and size you choose will depend on two primary factors:

- The number of employees or potential customers passing by the location daily
- The amount of competition nearby

If there are stands of bulk vendors in direct competition with each other, yours will draw more attention if they are more attractive. Charity sponsorships can make a substantial difference, since bulk vending customers are known to choose a charity machine over another nearby machine selling the same product without a charitable affiliation. Name-brand products are also proven to sell better in bulk vendors. When investigating the vending landscape, if the competition is selling chocolate-covered candies but not the actual brand, you can capture the market by filling your bulk vendor with real M&M'S chocolate, and in particular the peanut variety, which is one of the most popular bulk candies sold in vendors.

Because bulk vendors have been extremely popular with children, try to place at least some of your vendors at locations children and parents frequent, such as supermarkets, mall food courts, hair salons, game rooms, and sporting facilities. It is also a good idea to place them as close to the cashier or checkout stand as possible. Parents are more likely to have loose change to give to their children after making a purchase. Bulk vending machines are easy to service, requiring only about 15 or 20 minutes every one to two months.

How much money can you expect out of a bulk vendor every month? According to the 2008 edition of *Vending Times Census of the Industry*, the national average for the typical bulk vendor is 2.5 sales daily per individual machine compartment and $200 in gross profit per individual machine or compartment. So, if you have a three-headed bulk vendor bringing in an average of $200, you can gross at least $600 — leaving $500 as your own profit after subtracting product costs and other overhead expenses. While that might not seem like much, multiply that by 100 three-head bulk vendors; that is a $5,000 annual profit. Taking into account that you spend about 20 minutes every month or two restocking the machines, that $5,000 annually results in a nice hourly wage of $152. With a charity sponsorship (which regularly runs about $1 to $2 monthly) and only selling name-brand products, you could easily beat the national average and make even more.

The newest segment of the bulk vendor category is fun-size snack vending, which is the next-highest profit category of vending after bulk candy and nuts. Fun-size products include a variety of candy, nuts, and pretzels packaged in miniature or bite-size portions. These products are particularly attractive to consumers because of the individual packaging and wider variety of choices compared to traditional bulk vending. On average, they cost about 10 cents apiece and sell for about 25 cents; this represents a 250 percent markup. The new fun-size bulk vendors being developed can hold 200 to 250 items, but they cost more than a regular bulk vendor (around $200 to $275). Fun-size vendors tend to sell about 50 percent better than bulk machines, but hold less, so plan on servicing them roughly every two weeks. Vending just six times a day will produce about $17 in gross revenue monthly and a lower hourly wage — about $50 — because of increased servicing requirements, meaning you have to spend more of your time at locations.

Fun-Size Vendors: The Big Three

There are three basic types of fun-size vendors that can be found on the market today:

- Vertical stacking dispenser
- Flip-down shelf style
- Horizontal helix coil dispenser

The vertical stacking dispenser holds the highest volume of products, but it can be difficult to load and takes more time to restock. Although the flip-down shelf and the horizontal helix coil dispenser are much easier, both have a more limited product capacity compared to the vertical stacking dispenser.

It is easier to find locations for your fun-size machines, since the smaller portions cater more toward the trend of healthy eating habits. The bright, familiar packages also make for a nicer-looking display. Although you could also use a charity sponsorship to close the deal with a prospective location, managers are often satisfied with the attractive product display and convenience because there is no out-of-pocket cost for them. Aside from helping out a worthy cause, charity sponsorship makes locations easier to get, and it costs less than paying the location manager a commission. Although you can eventually customize the fun-size products according to the clientele and tastes of each individual location, start with top name brands, including M&M'S chocolate, Reese's® peanut butter cups, Skittles fruit-flavored sweets, and Butterfinger® candy bars.

For a high-traffic location where children frequent, such as a supermarket or shopping center, consider stocking some of your bulk vendors with stickers, temporary tattoos, or a variety of inexpensive toys that are sold in plastic capsules or eggs. These products are popular with children and parents — particularly for the parents who will be pleased to satisfy their child's craving for 50 cents or less.

Bulk vendors can also be adapted to vend trendier snacks and products. Buzz Bites® Chocolate Energy Chews (**www.vroom-foods.com**) is one type of product to recently hit the market, following the recent success of super-caffeinated energy drinks. A result of the partnership between Vroom Foods Inc. and Mad Dog Energy Products (**www.vroomfoods.com**), Buzz Bites contain 25 percent more caffeine than the leading energy drink and five B vitamins and ginseng. Buzz Bites vendors can also expect a 233 percent markup on their investment.

Snack and Beverage Vending

Snacks and beverages are the most popular vending sector, but they have the most competition since the higher price of the products provides a much larger profit margin for operators. You can find your own niche in this sector, though, if you are willing to offer good products and excellent customer service to the smaller companies (fewer than 100 employees, according to the SBA) that big operators tend to overlook. Your primary competition will be other small operators from whom you could win locations by offering newer machines or better product lines. You might also win their business by pricing products at least 10 percent lower than your competition; this is a perk that will benefit the entire company. A commission is also a tempting lure for locations, especially if their current vendor is not offering one. These can vary from 5 to 20 percent or higher, but try to keep it in the average range of 10 percent through negotiation. Any lower than that and you might insult the location owner. Any higher and you will be losing money. In any case, when you know you have competition, consider offering either the discount or the commission; never offer both unless you are absolutely sure of the location's earning potential.

Another way to win a location's snack and drink business is by studying what its current vendor is offering. If the location only has a soft drink machine with one product brand, they would most likely be interested in the option of offering multiple brands in one machine. You could then offer to stock both brands in your own machine(s), or even lease the competing bottler's machine if you only have a snack vendor and are short on funds to buy a new drink machine. Take note if the competitor's machines are mechanical or electronic. If they are mechanical or have older electronic machines, the location manager might be interested in having a newer, electronic machine with a built-in bill changer for the convenience of employees and customers.

Although you could simply concentrate on snack vending, most operators try to pair each snack machine with a cold drink machine, since customers buying a snack are also tempted to buy a drink to go along with it. There are machine distributors who sell paired snack and soda machines that operate the drink or the snack machine off the other machine's electronic circuitry and bill acceptor. Known in the industry as "slave" devices, these are a more economical option than buying two separate electronic machines with control panels and bill acceptors because less energy is used. There are compact units available that sell snacks and cold drinks in the same machine. These are excellent options for smaller companies and companies that are being upgraded from the honor system.

Snack and beverage machines will require more labor than bulk or honor vending systems. The extra work is found primarily in the time needed to restock and re-prioritize the products. They also have to be tended to more frequently — at least once or twice a month and perhaps more often, depending on the traffic in the location — but, the revenue stream is also larger. Based on a 20-employee company with little or no outside customer traffic, a combined snack and cold drink operation could provide from $200 to $250 in gross profit per month after discounting the cost of merchandise. The approximate gross profit of a snack vendor alone would be $100 after factoring in the cost of the products, and $120 to $140 for a cold-beverage machine only.

Just as in the bulk and fun-size snack categories, name-brand products will be your best bet for stocking your snack and cold-drink machines. People want to buy what they know. When in doubt about which snacks to stock, pay a visit to your local convenience store and ask the manager about the best-selling chips, crackers, and candies. You could also ask the advice of a vending machine operator in another city or state which products you should start out with in your snack vendors.

Full-Line Vending

As one of the most specialized sectors of vending, full-line vending adds the element of fresh and frozen foods to the vending repertoire. Most operators do not start out as full-line operators, but instead gradually grow into it as part of their customer service. The food choices in full-line vending can vary from salads and hot and cold sandwiches to popcorn, pizza, or French fries. It is a more complicated and labor-intensive business because extra precautions must be taken to ensure the machines are always stocked with fresh products. Every product has its own requirements for handling. However, there are a few guidelines to follow when dealing with fresh products. Candy items, in general, have expiration dates of six months to one year. Chips come in a bag with the expiration mark clearly stamped on it. Typically, the shelf life for chips is usually two to three months. The average shelf life for most fresh food products is seven days. Depending on the item, product shelf life can range anywhere from three days to three months. For this reason, full-line operators must make more frequent service calls to their machines than other vendors. Some vendors might even need to be managed daily. Because of the nature of this sector, full-line machines would only be economically feasible in the busiest of locations, which are those areas where no other food option is convenient — a classic example of this type of location is a manufacturing plant.

Hot beverage vending is also considered part of the full-line segment, and today it includes both vending machine beverages and office coffee service (OCS). In all but the largest locations, hot beverage vending has declined, with operators frequently removing the machines or replacing them with office coffee service. Locations usually pay a set fee for OCS. It is less labor intensive for operators and only requires a quality coffee maker instead of an expensive vending machine. Specialty coffee vendors that produce fresh cappuccino or espresso are the only coffee vendors that are seeing success in some markets, due to the popularity of these beverages.

South Florida equipment distributor VE South handles a large line of both countertop and freestanding specialty coffee vendors, and vice-president Joe Gilbert said his company's Brio and Colibri lines are taking the nation's coffee drinkers by storm. "We sell a coffee machine that is so popular across the county, it's hard to believe," he said. "You can put it up against any of the coffee shops on the market place. You can go in and get a cappuccino for a dollar, and it's the same quality — if not better — than what you'd pay $3 or $4 for in a specialty coffee shop."

Amusement Vending

This large sector of vending covers everything from video games and jukeboxes to kiddie rides and crane machines. A $7 billion per year industry, amusement vending offers huge profits. There is minimal labor, since there is no product to restock month after month, permits are not required, and operators do not have to collect and remit sales taxes. There are a few drawbacks. Many of the games and machines are very expensive, which requires larger start-up costs and more time to recoup the original investment. Repairs can be complicated on some of the more high-tech video games. It is also a more complicated form of vending, due to the increased competition, particularly in bars, taverns, and arcades. That can make locating this type of vendor even harder for operators without any prior sales or business negotiating experience. Paying commissions ranging from 20 to 50 percent is also common.

Although amusement arcades are the most visible form of this sector to the public, the 2008 edition of the *Vending Times Census of the Industry* reported almost half of all entertainment vendors are placed in bars, nightclubs, and taverns, with less than 20 percent placed in arcades. Because it is such a lucrative vending sector, most of these establishments are required to sign exclusivity contracts with one provider for all amusement machines. That means there is no room for most independent operators to get their foot in the door at larger establishments. Finding a business that is willing to host your machine is the most challenging aspect. Therefore, your primary task should be to conduct a comprehensive market research before you jump into the amusement-vending sector. Start locally and visit pubs, restaurants, bars, and cafes. You may find a high-profile location at a college or university. To help ensure consistent profit, purchase the most popular games that your budget can afford. For example, try to find games such as Pac-Man, Galaga, Asteroids, and Donkey Kong.

Bill Way, the author of *Vending Success Secrets* (**www.livefree. com**), said the easiest way for an amusement-vending entrepreneur to launch a business is to target retail establishments, such as restaurants and shopping centers. "The big operators just have too much overhead to concentrate on this type of location and need the big arcade, bar, and tavern locations to make the kind of money they want," he said.

Way warns new amusement operators from investing money in trendy video games that could potentially lose popularity in just a few months before the owners have a chance to recoup their original investment. Instead, he said operators should focus on multiple game devices or those that are "convertible" through the use of a new software cartridge. He also advises against investing in most of the larger games, such as kid rides, cranes, air hockey, pinball, pool tables, and electronic basketball "unless and until you really know what you are doing." Many of these large games require a substantial initial investment, and you may not have enough capital when you first start your business.

Often overlooked by the larger operators, there is a huge potential for success in the smaller, impulse vendor category of the amusement sector. Impulse vendors include such games as Memory Quiz, Love Meter, Talking Gypsy, and Stress Test. These are entertainment machines that do not require much time to play, making them perfect for places with high traffic and a number of people waiting, such as restaurants, airports, and shopping malls. Many are small enough to take with you when visiting a prospect's location. You can easily demonstrate how little room they require. Most are easy to set up and install, requiring only minimal programming.

Even after paying a 30-percent location commission, Way said it is common for the two-headed impulse machines to earn up to $42 per week or more, depending on the location. A new, two-headed machine will cost about $1,500, which he said can usually be recouped in six to 18 months. That results in a "much higher gross profit per hour" and less operator labor than traditional bulk vending. "This equates to about 60 percent to 200 percent gross-return per year," he said. "If you have substantial capital to invest but very little time, amusement may be ideal for you."

Making It Legal

Now that you have decided which business model to use, which vending approach to take, and how to pay for initial equipment and supplies, its time to take a deep breath, slow down, and make sure all bases are covered. First, find out if you can legally operate your new vending business out of your home, if that is your plan. For incorporated cities, call city hall and ask to be directed to the zoning and planning department; for unincorporated areas, the county government office is the place to begin. Your own neighborhood or community might have its own restrictions for home businesses as well, particularly if you live in a condominium development or a deed-restricted neighborhood. Some of these might even prohibit parking a service vehicle in the garage. If that is the case, rethink how and where you will need to base your vending business. This might require leasing a mini-storage unit or another warehouse facility.

Due to zoning restrictions, it may not be feasible to conduct business from your home. A quick way to assess this is to determine if the nature of your residence will change due the business activities. For example:

- What percentage of your house will be primarily for private residence or business?

- Will your business produce an increase in traffic or people working around the house?

- Will your business involve activities uncommon to a residential area?

- Will your business disturb neighbors due to noise levels or smells?

Once you determine the legality of running this business from your home, contact city, county, and state government tax collectors to find out what type of tax registration certificate you will need — more informally referred to as a business license. During the conversation, find out how your business will have to pay taxes to local municipalities. While you have the state office on the phone, ask about the forms and procedures for remitting sales taxes for the products you vend. You will need to secure a sales tax permit and whole tax number to use when purchasing stock so distributors, wholesale clubs, and other suppliers do not charge you sales tax.

Since you, as a vending operator, cannot collect sales taxes from your customers, you must pay them out of the profit earned on your merchandise if you are required to pay them. Figuring your sales taxes can become complicated if you operate in different municipalities with different taxing structures, but the sales tax return — sent to you by the city in which you filed —will guide you through the process. The tax return tells you the schedule of submission and walks you through a step-by-step filing process. Once you are issued a sales tax number, you will be told whether you must submit your sales taxes monthly, quarterly, or annually. Some states might require that you provide an advance deposit against your future sales taxes or a surety bond (a bond given to protect the recipient against loss in case the terms of contract are not fulfilled) from an insurance company. If you are unsure how to handle your sales taxes, seek professional advice from an accountant or bookkeeper.

Although you can legally operate a sole proprietorship under your own social security number, you might want to ask the Internal Revenue Service to issue you a tax identification number, which can be used for any phase of your business, even if you decide to one day take on a partner or incorporate. Once you have completed all the legal legwork for formalizing your new business, you will be ready to place your first vendors and jump into the daily rhythm of servicing a vending route.

Finding Your Own Vending Niche

The unique thing about the vending industry is that it offers the opportunity for entrepreneurs to sell just about anything they can find a market. Although not as varied as the Japanese market, which supports everything from bags of rice, piping hot canned breads, and even fingernail paintings, the vending market is growing in tandem with the ingenuity of its manufacturers and operators.

Wonderpizza

One of the most novel machines is one that vends freshly baked pizza. The Wonderpizza machine (**www.wonderpizzausa.com**), manufactured by the Italian firm Ironweld, produces a piping hot pizza in less than two minutes. The vendor is able to create and sell three different flavors of authentic crispy pizza due to its unique combination of a freezer unit and toaster oven in the same machine. This vending marvel is the result of five years of research and development. The machines can store up to 109 9-inch pizzas that sell for about $6 retail.

MooBella

Designed and manufactured in Massachusetts, MooBella® ice cream machines (**www.moobella.com**) first appeared in the Boston area in early 2008 as part of the company's test-marketing phase. "MooBella's patented process instantaneously aerates, flavors, and flash freezes the ingredients to produce a freshly made, delicious scoop of ice cream." Customers can create their own unique scoop of ice cream from both premium and light ingredients. There are up to 12 different flavors and three different toppings that can be mixed together. These unique vendors are currently only available in the New England area, and they are for rent rather than purchase.

Alcohol Alert

New roads are being made in the non-food areas of vending, as well. One new vending service, Alcohol Alert (**www.alcoholalert.com**), is providing breath analyzer machines for bars, nightclubs, and restaurants so patrons can know beforehand if they should attempt to drive or call a cab instead.

When Image is Everything

A European operator, The Beautiful Vending Company (**www. beautifulvending.com**), has found success in helping women keep beautiful hair, even in the most humid of climates. The company's vendors use high-temperature ceramic-plate irons to provide on-the-go hair straightening so women can have that just-styled look, even after visiting the gym or dancing the night away at a club. The machines are placed in ladies' rooms in restaurants, bars, health clubs, and other locales. Beautiful Vending is also looking to expand internationally, so these machines might be popping up in the United States soon.

The Dollar Massage Chair

You might find the perfect product for you in the amusement-vending sector. Massage chairs are a unique and fast-growing vendor because they can be placed in many locations that cannot afford to staff professional masseuse. These locations include barbershops, beauty salons, shopping centers, airports, waiting rooms at medical clinics, and others. Most of the public has seen these types of chairs demonstrated at trendy stores, such as The Sharper Image, but few people want to shell out the bucks to have their own at home. The comfortable and relaxing chairs are particularly a temptation when a customer can get a three-minute massage for just $1. The Dollar Massage Chair by Massage Manufacturers Direct Inc. (**www.dollar-massage.com**) features a preset massage that kneads, rolls, and taps your back. The chair features a vibrating footrest and might well be the best way to take a load off your feet when you are about to drop from shopping.

Chapter Takeaways

Vending is no different than any other business. The keys to success are starting small, keeping things as simple as possible, and growing slowly. Refer to this chapter often to learn the pros and cons of the various types of vending options. From honor-system snack and drink systems, bulk vending, snack and beverage vending, full-line vending, and amusement vending, you have a good selection from which to choose.

- An honor snack system is a cardboard or plastic box with dividers for different types and sizes of snacks, along with an attached coin or cash box

- Bulk vending machines offer the highest profit margins in the industry; they are also inexpensive to launch and easy to service

- Since bulk vendors are extremely popular with children, try to place at least some of your vendors where children and parents frequently visit — malls, supermarkets, game rooms, and sporting facilities

- There are three basic types of fun-size vendors on the market today: vertical stacking dispensers, flip-down shelf styles, and horizontal helix coil dispensers

- Snacks and beverages are the most popular vending sector, but have the most competition

- As one of the most specialized sectors of vending, full-line vending adds the element of fresh and frozen foods to the vending repertoire

- As a $7 billion per year industry, amusement vending offers huge profits with minimal labor involved

CHAPTER 8

Servicing Your Machines

As previously mentioned, the amount of time you spend servicing the vending machines on your route varies according to several factors: the style and number of machines, driving distance to and from the locations, and the distance from your vehicle to the vending area. Bulk and fun-size machines take less time to service than an honor system box or full-size snack vendor. Machines offering cold drinks will also take more time since the cases must be stacked on a dolly for transport into the facility for loading.

Service Must-Haves

An important investment for servicing vendors on a route should be a sturdy dolly or hand truck, preferably one that can be transformed into a four-wheel cart for the bulky or heavier loads. What this will cost — on average between $59.95 and $209.95 — will save a lot of wear and tear on your back, especially if you plan to vend cold drinks. To protect candies and other perishables from the summer heat, invest in a few heavy-duty ice chests: a larger one for the majority of your stock and a smaller, handheld model to carry bulk candies.

Full-size soda and snack machines stock either from top to bottom or back to front. This ensures that older products sell before those added more recently. While restocking, remove any products that are close to or have passed their expiration dates. Keep track of these on your notebook later for use with your profit and loss sheet at income tax time.

Wipe down or clean all machines with an all-purpose cleaner. Test the coin and bill acceptors to ensure they work properly. Once finished, make a test purchase from each row or shelf of a machine to make sure the products dispense properly. Some modern electronic vendors have a test mode that will cycle through a test vend of each product. A moved or shifted vendor might be a sign of a disgruntled customer who may have tilted or banged on the machine because it was not dispensing, so check thoroughly to verify merchandise is flowing and change is being returned to customers.

After you have stocked and cleaned your machines, remove the money for counting and later depositing. This is a simple process for bulk machines, which do not require coins to make change. Empty the coin box in the back or bottom of the unit and replace it securely, making sure it is locked. Removing the money in mechanical snack and drink machines that do not make change is a similar process.

Emptying the funds from electronic vendors and those that make change is a little more complicated. To start, empty the dollar bills from the bill acceptor. Next, remove the coins found in the coin box, which is where the machine stores extra coins when the coin tubes are full. Finally, ensure that the coin tubes are still full so they have sufficient money for making change. While performing these steps, clean the bill validator with a special alcohol-soaked pad made for this purpose. This will ensure the vendor's bill mechanism will not reject dollar bills — a major frustration to customers with no change. Before leaving each machine, check to see whether the locks on the coin box and the front of the machine are secure.

Keep the money from individual machines separate so you can compare sales to previous visits. The best way to do this is with sturdy bank deposit bags, which can be kept with you at all times when servicing a location. If you have multiple machines in a particular location, separate the proceeds into individual, small plastic bags marked with the name of the machine within the bank bag. Using a different bank bag for each location is another way to keep the monies separate. To protect your profits further, consider having a strongbox or safe bolted to the floor of your delivery vehicle, if feasible. That way, you can deposit your proceeds into the safe between service calls and leave them locked up in your driveway without fear of theft.

Routine Service For Your Machines is a Must

Provide regular service on bulk vendors once every two months, and fun-size machines once a month, due to a more limited capacity. Honor systems will require at least biweekly visits depending on sales. Maintain snack and beverage machines every week or two, according to the requirements of the individual locations. For locations where you sell a lot of perishable goods, such as pastries, you should stop by at least weekly to ensure the machines remain stocked with fresh products. If the perishables are slow sellers, replace them with other items and reduce the service frequency. The service schedule on your beverage vendors will depend on the machine capacity and seasonal changes; cold drinks tend to sell faster during the warm summer months. You might even find that certain high-volume locations around hotel or apartment building swimming pools will require service more than once a week to keep the machine from running out of drink selections.

If possible, maintain vending machines during off-peak hours (typically between 9 p.m. and 7 a.m.) so you do not interfere with employees and customers on their lunch or coffee breaks. To save time and travel expenses, you should only service them when absolutely necessary. For this reason, it is best to carry a small notebook with you when servicing your route to jot down details about each vending location. By taking careful notes, you will soon discover which items are consistently running out, which ones are slow sellers, and which ones can be deleted from future inventories. Comparing notes can also help determine if you need to increase or decrease the frequency of service calls to a particular location. Many operators use what are known as route cards or delivery receipts for this purpose. These are pre-printed forms, which operators fill out for each vendor after servicing. When you are back in the office, transfer the information from the route cards to a computer spreadsheet to help keep track of sales trends and figures. By studying the numbers, shifting products around, and adding more of the popular items, you might be able to drop weekly calls at some locations to every other week.

To avoid fumbling with a new vendor in public and risk looking like a novice to the location manager, learn how to efficiently stock your machines before you place them. In your garage or workshop, take the machine out of its factory packaging and set it up. With the owner's manual in hand, go through the vendor loading directions step-by-step. Practice loading each shelf and line until you can repeat the process smoothly. This way, if you run into any snags, it will be in the privacy of your garage rather than facing the world in your trial-and-error stage.

Machine delivery and setup

Regardless of the method used to find a particular location, make a personal site visit to conduct a final assessment of feasibility of having machines there and determine vendor placement. Unless you are planning on delivering the vendor(s) personally or accompanying the contracted delivery crew, perform a site survey of the location. If you are personally delivering the vendor(s), be sure to measure door- and entryways to decide the best — and easiest — route to use. During a personal visit to the location, take a notebook, writing instrument, and tape measure to jot down all the pertinent details. Here are some things to consider while assessing a location, and before making the delivery of your machines:

- Make sure there is an electrical outlet nearby if you are using electronic machines or mechanical vendors with illumination

- Ensure the machine(s) will be in a visible, high-traffic location

- If you are not completely satisfied with the placement area during the visit, speak with the location manager to see if you can find a more suitable spot

- If you are hiring movers to bring in your vendor(s), draw a detailed map, including the measurements of doorways and distances from the entryway to the placement site

- If you own a digital camera, it is a good idea to take several photos of the location and print them out or have them processed at a one-hour photo service to give to the movers

- Verify how close you will be able to park a delivery vehicle to facilitate the process

Even if you plan to move your own machines once in a while, it is a good idea to develop a good relationship with some local movers who can help you with the larger vendors. Although you might consider hiring some local college students who would do the job for less money, unless you have access to the proper equipment, it would be better to hire professionals who are used to hauling machines of that weight and size. They generally are more careful, and less likely to hurt themselves since they perform this type of work on a regular basis. Most professional movers have liability insurance to cover accidents and injuries.

If you plan on doing the moving yourself, you will need a proper moving vehicle. Use a heavy-duty pickup truck if you have access to one. Get some sort of ramp to move the machine onto and out of the truck bed. Use extreme caution when moving heavy vendors. If you own an open-top flatbed trailer, that will also work because it is usually lower to the ground than the back of a pickup truck. Invest in sturdy ratcheting straps to secure the machines during transit. Find a specialized lift or jack to cart vendors into your locations. A pallet jack, a tool or machine used to lift pallets, can be used for machines with legs, but use another type of lift for vendors with low ground clearance, such as cold-drink machines.

Without access to your own moving vehicle, the next best bet is to rent a moving truck from one of the household moving companies. Renting one with a built-in hydraulic lift gate will make your work that much easier and only cost slightly more.

Maintaining the Relationship

Checking in with your location manager from time to time is one of the best ways to ensure customer satisfaction and keep competitors from honing in on your territory. Popping in to say a quick hello, asking for any particular requests, and offering a free snack or cold drink is an inexpensive form of public relations that goes a long way in customer retention. You might even consider throwing a pizza party or bringing in doughnuts once a year as a "thank you" for the location's business. Use the time you are bringing in the goodies to chat with the staff and identify their vending preferences.

Bill Way, author of *Vending Success Secrets*, said "attitude is everything" when it comes to route management and keeping locations. "Be sure and watch your attitude when servicing your route," he wrote. "Take time to say 'Hi' to people; ask, 'How's the service?' or 'What would you like to see in the machine?' Hand out a sample or two and be friendly. In short: Be noticed and be liked. You'll never have to worry about keeping the location."

Refund policies should be clear

Minimize problems for your location managers by clearly stating the refund policy on all machines. The last thing you want is for them to call you for every complaint. Ensure that your contact phone number and refund information is visible on the machine near the bill or coin receptors. If you have a problematic machine, be sure to change it out quickly. This prevents the loss of the location where too many patrons are losing money in your machine. People will quickly stop using a machine if it consistently eats their money and does not vend a product — losing $1 once is one thing; losing $1 each time the machine is used really adds up.

Way said that a lot of vending operators try to protect their privacy by not putting their home phone numbers on their vendors, which he insisted is not good for business. For those operators, he recommended obtaining an inexpensive private voice mailbox that works just like an answering service so location managers can contact them, if necessary. "You need to be reachable if a machine malfunctions, runs out of product, business location is closing down, etc.," he said. "If you want to stay in business and prosper, you must offer good service. Good service starts with being accessible."

With any location where you have vendors, you and the location manager must decide on a workable refund policy that is reasonable for both of you — this is a mutually beneficial relationship. This will depend on the size of the company and whether there is a staff available to issue refunds and gather vending machine information. There are several ways to handle refunds, all of which should make use of pre-printed refund slips.

Have these refund slips produced at a printer, or design and print them yourself with your home computer. Place the name of your company in bold letters at the top of the coupon so it stands out from the rest of the text on the page. This will not only distinguish your machines and your refunds from competitors, but will also reinforce your brand and create a good reputation for your company with respect to customer service. Other essential elements on the slip include space for:

- Customer's name
- Date
- Item purchased or attempted to purchase
- Location of the machine
- Refund amount requested and the reason

By analyzing this information, you can determine what part of which machines are problematic and need attention or repair.

Outsource your refund processing

The most popular method for handing out refunds is to have an office administrator handle this responsibility. Supply this person with a small amount of cash in bills and coins, either $10 or $20, depending on the size of the location. The administrator should hand out and collect refund slips. This individual can also ensure the slips are properly filled out with all the necessary information.

The less preferred method is to hang a pair of manila envelopes or plastic bags on the side of your vendors, with one marked "blank refund slips, and the other marked "completed refund slips." Whenever someone arrives to service your vendors, check the bag for any completed refund slips and take these with you when you leave. Once you arrive back at your office, separate cash for each refund and place it in a separate envelope marked with the name of the individual requesting the refund. These are then turned in to the person in charge of distributing refunds at the location. When checking on the refund situation each time you visit, be sure to hand out a free snack or a cold drink. This will go a long way to making your refund process smooth and almost painless.

Vending operators with machines that accept dollar bills are beginning to issue coupons rather than cash refunds. Using coupons is a way to ensure the money remains in your machine rather than being used in another vendor owned by a different company. Since the bill acceptor can usually be adjusted to read coupons, operators know they will see the value refunded in their machines.

Keep Your Vendors Vending

Maintenance and repair are key factors to any vending operation. Minor problems are commonplace in the industry, ranging from jammed coin mechanisms to stubborn bill acceptors and damaged machine spirals. Major problems, such as break-ins, drilled locks, and vandalism can quickly put you out of commission, especially without having a dedicated, reliable repairman available. Even the most non-mechanically inclined vending operators need to buy a simple tool kit and learn the basics, particularly preventative maintenance, to keep their businesses running smoothly.

The first step is to familiarize yourself with your vendors. If you have not done so already, pull out the owner's manuals since you will be referring to them often, especially for minor repairs and troubleshooting tips. If you did not get a manual with your used vendor, try to find one for free through the manufacturer's Web site. These Web sites frequently have a link to owner's manuals, which are listed by model name or number. If yours is unavailable through the manufacturer, you might still be able to find it online for a fee through a private company. Consult electronic vendors' manuals for directions on how to program pricing and other features. The more you learn about your vendors, the more money you can save on repairs by being able to accurately describe the problem to a repairman.

Due to the nature of their simplistic design, bulk vendors rarely require maintenance, unless a coin gets jammed in the coin slot or a product gets jammed in the delivery shaft. You can do some simple preventative maintenance on the coin slot and turn handle by applying a few drops of machine oil or spraying with WD-40® spray, inserting coins a few times, and working the mechanism. Each time you service the machine, carefully examine the delivery shaft for any foreign objects and perform a few test vends to ensure that the vendor is operating correctly.

The coin mechanism can also be another source of simple problems in mechanical vending machines. Occasionally pull out and clean the coin mechanism to reduce the possibility of future jams, followed by several test vends to ensure it is working properly. One way to become familiar with the inner workings of a mechanical machine is to simply open the service door, deposit coins, and make selections; watch what actions must take place to vend.

Although electronic vendors by nature are more complicated, it is important to become acquainted with the coin mechanism, bill acceptor, and vend motors. Once again, you can do a test vend with the service door open to watch the vendor go through the vending motions. The bill validator is also an area that performs better with regular maintenance. Clean the device regularly with a specially designed alcohol pad. The pad is inserted as a dollar bill to clean any grime that is built up. After ensuring no bills are stuck inside the bill acceptor, test it a few times before leaving.

Have your repairperson on speed dial

Develop a good working relationship with a vending repairperson so you can contact him or her on short notice to help solve a machine malfunction. Each time you use this repairperson, carefully watch how he or she works and note the steps performed. Write down the details of what was done for future reference. That way, if the same problem occurs again or on another machine, you can try to fix the problem yourself before incurring the expense of another service call.

Taking a course on professional repairs would also be a good idea to help save money on maintenance. Check with the *Vending Times* (**www.vendingtimes.com**) and National Automatic Merchandising Association (NAMA), or go online to find vending repair courses offered in your area. The more repairs you are able to perform by yourself, the more of your hard-earned money stays in your pocket. One of the first things Bruce Adams of Rainbow Vending Inc. did after founding his company in 1995 was take a vending machine repair course. He now handles most of the repairs on his machines, although he said he also decided to go with one particular vendor company years ago for additional help on larger, more complex repairs, and because they offered toll-free technical support.

It is always a good idea to have a good vending repairperson on your speed dial, even if you do some of your own repairs. To find vending machine repairpersons in your area, check out **www.vendingconnection.com** and click on the "Parts, Repair Service" link. There, you will find links to vending machine parts, equipment parts, vending parts supplier companies, and vending repair services.

Chapter Takeaways

To be a successful vending machine operator, you will need fully functional vending machines, which require regular, consistent maintenance and servicing. This maintenance includes delivery, set up, stocking, cleaning, counting money, refund processing, and repairs. Here are a few key points to remember about service for your machines:

- Learn to efficiently stock your machines before you place them at a location

- Make personal site visits to conduct final assessments of the location for traffic, vendor placement, and access for maintenance, servicing, and stocking

- Minimize problems with your location managers by clearly stating your refund policy on the vendors

- Keep commonplace vending problems to a minimum by purchasing a simple tool kit and learning the basics

- Gather owner's manuals for all of your vending machines and make sure they are easily accessible

- The more you learn about your machines, the more money you can save on repairs

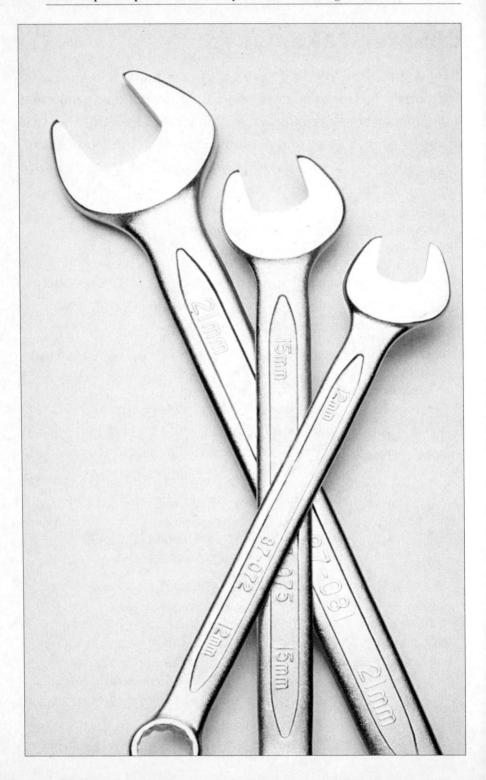

CHAPTER 9

Merchandising and Inventory Control

As far as the financial success of your vending company goes, this is where the rubber meets the road. But, if you have never managed a snack machine, how will you know what to stock? This is where your own product distributors can give you a hand, since they will also have a vested interest in your success in the hope of repeat sales. They can help you decide what percentages of various products with which to fill your snack vendors. Granted, each region of the country and specific locations will have variations according to tastes and seasons, but Five Star Distributors Inc. of Chicago recommends stocking a 654-product snack vendor in the following proportions:

- 54.1 percent candy and snack bars
- 15.3 percent with mints and gums
- 9.2 percent with pastries
- 7.65 percent of a variety of salty snacks
- 6.1 percent with large single-portions of salty snacks

If you are going with a product distributor, ask your representative to help you break down your own size vendor into approximate percentages. If you are going to rely on warehouse-type stores and other suppliers, use the same percentages listed above and adjust them to your individual location's preferences as you go.

According to *Vending Times*, the inventory control system, known as category management, is now being widely used in the vending world to help operators stock their vendors with the products that sell well. Using category management for snack vendors, businesses should divide products into three distinct categories: core, cycle, and choice. This was validated by a market research performed by the Nabisco Inc. snack food company.

Core items will occupy 20 percent of your vendors' available space. These items are the ones you will consistently stock. Cycle the items you will stock every day in every vendor for specific periods of time; these should take up about 60 percent of your vendors' available space. These consist of the top brands in every category, items for a variety of tastes, and hot new products. Choice items are products you provide for an individual location based on special requests by employees or location managers to bring up your sales numbers in that particular area. According to Nabisco, choice items should be restricted to no more than three items.

Make Your Planogram Work for You

Using a planogram — a diagram that depicts how and where products should be displayed on a shelf to increase customer purchasing — can help guide you in proper product selection. A planogram can be hand-drawn or created using specific computer software programs; RouteSail® Millennia is an example of a popular planogram application. The elements that go into a planogram feature the machine's exact number of columns, shelves, or rows, and also total capacity. With a properly filled-out planogram for each location, there will never be a doubt as to how to fill a particular vendor. Even with the use of such planning devices, owners of successful vending companies say products should be switched around periodically in the machine from one spiral or shelf to another. This trick has been known to improve sales in slower-moving items, since customers who always make the same selections frequently choose another when they cannot find their favorite in its usual spot.

Learning to stock cold-drink machines is not quite as complicated due to the more limited number of selections and the commonplace practice of using bottler-leased vendors. When using machines supplied by a bottler, you still must decide what kinds of drinks to stock, but that particular bottler must supply them all. Depending on the size of the machine, decide on up to eight product choices. Once again, your bottler representative can offer advice or suggestions on how to divide up your leased vendor. When you start operating, assess each individual location for customer preferences. Due to the limited number of beverage slots, limit special requests to no more than one or two choices, and change those up every few months according to sales.

If you are going with your own cold-drink vendors, choose any variety of drinks you want, even personally customizing them for specific locations. For example, offering more fruit and energy drinks at hospitals, gymnasiums, and schools would be wise. Be cautious with your choices if you are operating with one of the drink machines with fewer selections. For these, stick with the most popular soft drinks.

Modern vending machines now use telemetry, a wireless Internet connection that notifies vending operators when a machine is running low or is out of a particular product. The vendor can be programmed to send the information to any e-mail address so operators can receive the information by cell phone or personal computer. This technology is now helping operators avoid missed sales during high-volume sales periods.

It is All About Your Products

There are several options for finding the products you need to fill your vending machines. Your choice will depend on the size of your business and the amount of time you invest in scanning the market for the best prices. Operators just starting out will find it easy to get wholesale prices on certain products by joining a members-only wholesale club, such as Sam's Club or BJ's Wholesale Club. These stores are useful when you need merchandise in a pinch, but prices are slightly more than what distributors offer. Selections might vary, and you might not be able to find certain niche market products at these stores. Wholesale clubs are not the best choice for cold-drink purchases unless you only need canned beverage as the stock.

Wholesale distributors will be your most dependable source for the largest variety of products, since these companies buy directly from the manufacturer and offer some of the lowest prices available. There are also a number of distributors that specialize in supplying products for the vending industry, and many can be found by a simple Internet search. *Also, reference Appendix B for a listing of a few product sources.* Your area's snack food distributors are another option, particularly if you do not want to buy huge quantities of a particular item. These route salespeople will even deliver to your home or warehouse. If you do not have any luck locating them in the phone book or on the Internet, head to your local convenience store, ask for the telephone number of their distributing company, or wait for the distributor's employees to show up.

For cold drinks, your best bet would be your local soft drink bottler. These bottlers offer the widest selection and best price, although they require the purchase of a minimum number of cases per order. They will also deliver directly to your home or warehouse, which is another advantage if you are strapped for time.

Most distributors and bottlers offer payment terms to those companies that qualify. In general, they offer 30 days net to approve companies, which means you have 30 days from the time the products are invoiced and shipped to pay the bill without penalty. If you do not have a good credit record or are a new company starting out, they might require cash terms until they are satisfied that you are a stable business and in the game for the long haul. Whichever source you choose for your merchandise starting out, you will probably eventually find you get your best variety of products by buying from a mixture of these sources based on your particular preference and experience.

Before ordering merchandise for your vendors, decide how you are going to store the products so you will have some place to receive them when they are delivered. Many small operators begin by working out of a car or van and use their garage or a spare bedroom to store the stock. This is a good system while your business is still growing. It is easy to control the temperature in your home to protect candies from melting in the summer and perishables from spoiling. Once your business grows and you begin to receive large vending units on a regular basis, begin looking for a larger storage facility.

One of the least expensive options for additional storage is a mini-storage unit. These come in various sizes, capable of holding just a few items to holding a houseful of belongings. Mini-storage units are often conveniently located in many neighborhoods and next to major highways, so you should not have to drive far to get to your stored merchandise. You will, of course, need to select one that is climate-controlled, unless you plan on discontinuing the sale of chocolate in the warmer months. These types of facilities are usually secure, with controlled access gates, security cameras, and sometimes 24-hour security personnel. Even with all this, still invest in a top-quality padlock that is resistant to bolt cutters and saws to protect your investment.

You can also opt for professional warehousing facilities, which cost a bit more. Most of these are climate-controlled and can be rented with or without warehouse services, depending on your need. If you opt for a larger warehouse or mini-storage unit, you will be wise to also invest in a few key pieces of warehouse equipment, such as shelving, a pallet jack, a dolly or hand cart, and a trash and recycling container for your discarded packaging materials.

As in any other product business, the objective in vending is to sell what you buy. It is also crucial to have it in stock to sell, but if merchandise is sitting too long on your warehouse floor, it is taking up space and funds that could be put to better use. The hard part of inventory management is finding that perfect balance in keeping merchandise flowing through your warehouse and machines without staying too long or running out in either place. Fortunately, you can learn from others who have gone before you down the path of inventory control and employ some of their tricks and techniques.

Many businesses use what is called a "par sheet" to keep track of in-stock merchandise and that which needs to be ordered. A par sheet is an inventory sheet listing each of your products and the current amount on hand, as well as how much you need to order now and from whom in order to keep from running out. The "par" is the predetermined number your stock must fall below before you reorder the same product or products.

For simplicity's sake, say you are a bulk-vending operator who has 50 double-headed vendors already placed in thriving locations. One side vends gumballs and the other nuts or candy, depending on the clientele. Each 850-count bag of gumballs will fill the gumball side of your vendors almost twice, so 25 bags of gumballs would fill each of your 50 gum vendors and leave you enough reserve stock for the next restocking in two months or so. You have already determined that you should reorder 12 bags of gumballs when you are down to about 13 in stock. So, for gumballs, 13 would be your par number. Once you begin to fall below that amount, your order should be in the processing stage or already completed.

Then, say the other side of your 12-pound capacity vendors is divided equally between cashews, which come in 20-pound bags, and chocolate candy, which come in 35-pound cases. To initially fill up your machines, you will need 300 pounds each of cashews (15 bags) and chocolate candy (about eight and one-half bags). Since you should always have enough stock to fill your vendors at least half full, eight bags should be your par for cashews and five cases should be your par for chocolate candy.

Practice makes perfect

You will have to order stock more often for your snack vendors and cold-drink machines. Finding the par number for each item or beverage will take a little practice. A good rule of thumb is to have enough stock on hand to fill every row, slot, or shelf of your vendors when placing your next order. If you are tight on funds to begin, wait to order until you only have enough merchandise on hand to fill the vending machines half-full. You might have to revisit your vendors sooner than planned to make sure they have not gotten too low, but you will ensure the machines are not running on empty. The route cards, briefly mentioned in Chapter 8, will also help you determine which items are selling the most in each location to determine how much your par should be for each individual item. If you do not already have them, a personal computer and an inventory software program would be good investments. Some programs might even notify you when you reach your par on items and compile a "to order" list for you.

Most beverage bottlers and other distributors take orders and deliver weekly, but also require receipt of your order by a certain day of the week. If you miss a week and need a certain item, your easiest recourse will be at one of the previously mentioned warehouse clubs. Although you might pay slightly more, they are great resources for last-minute purchases and are usually open until 9 p.m.

Delivery instructions for product distributors are crucial if you are servicing your machines and no one else is available to receive your shipments. Work out a plan with the drivers beforehand on how and where they can safely leave shipments if you are unavailable. It is important to carefully compare packing slips with invoices, even if you are present for the deliveries. Be sure to note any discrepancies and notify the distributor as soon as possible.

Protecting Your Products

If you are going to be a snack vendor, find ways to help your products stay fresh and protected from spoilage as long as possible. The best way to ensure this is to be cautious about buying anything on special. Anytime a distributor is offering you a truly good deal, it is for a reason. It is possible the company purchased too much of a product and is offering you the savings to help liquidate it. Then again, the product could be nearing the end of its expiration date. To find the real reason behind the special, ask the right questions. Is the product being discontinued? Is the product past its expiration date? Is there an overstock on the item? If the product is nearing its expiration date, you will have to decide if you can move it quickly enough without eating it — literally.

The last thing you want as a vendor is to develop the reputation of stocking stale or old snacks. This can cripple sales after just a few instances and can cause you to lose a good location. And do not forget the power of word-of-mouth. If you are constantly stock stale items at one location, chance are good that the word will get out to other locations where you have machines. That is the reason you must always pull snacks out of your machines before they go out of date. Pay particular attention to pastries and doughnuts, which have a much shorter shelf life than other items. If you find they are not moving quickly enough, stock fewer of them and fill the rest of the row with other snacks, or remove them altogether. You will develop better public relations by handing them out as freebies to workers than by taking a chance on somebody spending money on a stale product. In the worst-case scenario, they can be listed as waste and used as a write-off at income tax time.

One way you can help speed up the sale of products nearing their expiration dates is by the selective use of sales and promotions. For example, you can do a "Frivolous Friday" sale each week and offer one or two items for half price or less. It is important to place neatly lettered signs on your vendors that announce the sale in a big way. If you alternate the types of products, your customers might never realize why you are doing it. Once you experiment with sales and learn how to succeed with them, take advantage of those specials offered by your distributor. Just be sure you can still make a profit when taking the sale price into account.

Protect your snacks against the harmful effects of summer heat and humidity. Whether you keep your snacks and drinks in a warehouse, the garage, or a spare bedroom of your home, take steps to ensure merchandise is stored in a dry place away from direct sunlight. Take specific precautions with candies, especially the chocolates. Although cold temperatures are not so much a problem, a summer heat wave could prove devastating to your chocolate stock. If your garage or warehouse is not air-conditioned, you must find a way to refrigerate your chocolates, either by investing in a used refrigerator or moving them into your home for the summer.

Chocolates must also be protected in transit, since temperatures in a parked vehicle can soar in the summer. Invest in a large ice chest for your delivery vehicle and keep it cool with refreezable plastic ice substitutes. Keep in mind that certain chocolate candy with a harder outer shell might not melt, but the candy shells can become soft and can be damaged in transit.

Since your snack vendors are not refrigerated, do not place them in the direct sunlight or next to any equipment that releases heat. If your machines are located outdoors, either stop stocking chocolates in the summer or request the management provide an air-conditioned spot, at least for a few months. Most managers will do their best to accommodate if they realize there will be no more chocolate, since chocolate is a popular vending choice.

If you are a bulk vendor selling nuts in the hot and humid south, you will also need to protect your stock. Although heat might not be such a problem, dampness is. It would be best to refrigerate all of your back stock of nuts, at least until the humidity index dies down. Also, try to make sure your machines are not in direct sunlight or exposed to the elements. If that is unavoidable, swap out the nuts and the chocolate until the cooler weather returns.

Bringing Up Sales

Unlike the direct sale of goods and services from one person to another, vending machine operators cannot rely on a fast-talking sales pitch to close the deal. Instead, they must rely on their machines to do all the talking, and non-verbal clues can make or break your vending business. A machine that is dusty, dingy, or dirty is basically sending the message that nobody wants what it has to offer. A machine with a jammed bill receptor and an illuminated "no change" light will also turn off potential customers. For this reason, it is imperative for machines to be kept clean and in good working order.

You should also try to fill your vendors as full as possible. Nothing hurts sales more than a machine with just a few items remaining, which is basically telling passers-by that the merchandise is old and picked over. If you are just starting out and cannot afford to fill your vendors completely, it is better to make more frequent visits to your locations and use the proceeds to buy more merchandise than to miss sales from the lack of product availability.

One way to bring up sales in any given location is to attempt to customize vendors to particular locations and customer requests. If you notice the chips are sold out each time you visit a particular location, begin stocking at least two rows or shelves of that product each visit. If the item continues to keep selling out, consider expanding to more rows. This is where you will need to refer back to your route cards to decide which other products in this particular vendor are the slowest sellers. To find the extra space for more high-selling snacks, combine the two slower sellers on the same row or shelf. The best way to do this might be to alternate the two products so each sale of one brings the other to the forefront.

Know your users

Try to get an accurate picture of the each location's demographics, either by asking the manager or making a visual estimate yourself. Are there more females than males? If so, add more diet soft drinks to your cold beverage vendor and more non-fat or healthier snack alternatives, such as granola bars and a bigger variety of baked chips, to your snack vendor because women statistically eat healthier than men. Seventy percent of women (compared to 60 percent of men) try to eat fewer calories in the day. If you are a full-line vendor, you many need to place more yogurt and salad options in your machine, or a healthier variety of ice cream. Not being able to meet the demands of your users can reflect negatively on your locations, and once again, that information can quickly spread to your other locations. If your vendors are in an industrial area or automotive repair facility, chances are pretty good that the majority of employees will be male. In that case, one row of diet drinks would probably be sufficient for employees and any outside customer traffic, but you might want to consider adding a row of sports or energy drinks if you have the space. A more popular vending choice for such an environment might be a bigger variety of salted nuts, flavored snack crackers, and chips.

Although it is not always possible to please everyone, do your best to fulfill special customer requests, even if it is just half a row or shelf of the requested product to see how it sells. By alternating the product with another one, the requested product will always be no more than a sale away from the person who requested it and might prompt the sale of the other product to get to the desired one. For example, if you only have one row or shelf devoted to pastries, and one customer has asked for cupcakes, try alternating cupcakes with the pastries to see how that arrangement works. Special promotions are a way to increase product interest and awareness, as well as offer your customers special values from time to time. Your product distributors or sales representatives can supply you with see-through plastic stickers known as "static clings," which you can use to promote a particular product every week or two, and even announce special prices.

Consider prizes and giveaways

Another way to increase sales is through the use of cash prizes or giveaways, via the use of stickers adhered to certain product packages in your vendors. Develop a cooperative relationship with the location receptionist or manager to whom customers could go to redeem the prizes. Once the relationship is in place, use stickers to award everything from sports tickets and movie passes to free products. This option would work best in an office environment rather than public vending area; however, in public vending machines, prizes could come directly from the manufacturer. In locations without someone willing to be the redeemer, tape cash prizes to the back of certain packages. The chance to win something for free is always a great hook, and you might even find the increased sales more than cover the cost of the promotion. Make use of the static clings or other attention-getting methods for the giveaways to bring more action to your vendors.

Since most bill receptors can also accept a variety of vending machine coupons, operators with bill-receptor machines can give a limited amount of coupons good for a free product every so often to a particular location to create a good rapport with customers. The managers can then use them as employee perks for meeting specific goals or above-average performance.

A more costly option to attract attention to your vendor is to set it on "free vend" during a specific period, such as during an important employee or sales meeting. This method specifically creates good will between the operator and the location manager, but should be used sparingly since attendees can take as much as they want during the event. Place attractive signs on your vendor during the event announcing, "Snacks and beverages courtesy of ABC Vending." Customers will remember your generosity. Above all, remember to visit and restock the machine and to turn off the free vend as soon as the meeting ends. If you happen to forget, contact the location manager to have him or her turn it off.

To further increase product sales, swap out the slowest sellers from your vendors from time to time to try another item or brand. This way, you will eventually find the perfect mix of products for each individual location.

Moving Your Stock

Now that you have decided what you are going to vend, you should decide what kind of vehicle would work for your business. Unless you plan on staying a small-time operator, you might find it difficult to work outside of the trunk and backseat of an automobile. Although the family car might work fine for just starting out, you might find that it does not hold enough merchandise to adequately finish servicing your route before having to return home or to the warehouse to restock the vehicle. This might end up costing more time and fuel in the long run than the price of a larger service vehicle.

No matter what type of vehicle you settle on, outfit it with a safe or strong box bolted to the floor to protect the cash profits you collect daily from your vending operation. These usually come with a mechanical or digital combination, the latter requiring much more time to crack than a standard dial combination. Although you will be using lockable zippered cash pouches to transport your proceeds from the locations to your service vehicle, immediately transfer the money into the securely locked safe in your service vehicle, so as not to leave your profits unattended. Consider investing in heavy-duty commercial locks for your vending vehicle, which will deter all but the most determined of thieves.

It is also imperative to notify your insurance company that you are driving a vehicle for commercial purposes; the rates will be higher than a general personal policy, but you will not run the risk of your company refusing to pay an accident claim later. Shop around for the best rates on a business liability insurance policy for your vending operation. Many locations require vendors to have such protection before working on the premises, and a good policy will protect you in the event a vendor falls on someone while tipping the machine to get to a jammed product.

Minivans and cargo vans

Most vending operators find a cargo van to be the most efficient and economical solution to servicing their routes. The size van you need will depend on the current size and scope of your vending route and possible future expansion. If you plan on servicing just a few locations per day, a minivan might be your best solution. Most minivan models come in a cargo version, which is preferable for business use, although a passenger model could serve double duty simply by removing the rear seat for route servicing and putting the rear seat back for your everyday car use.

If you plan on servicing more locations daily or prefer to maintain some stock permanently in your service vehicle, opt for a full-size cargo van. These not only provide more cubic feet of storage space, but are also roomy enough for keeping a hand-cart onboard, which is extremely important for cold-drink vending and hauling small vendors in need of servicing. Since these vehicles are usually outfitted with a six-cylinder engine and offer eight-cylinder options, they also make better towing vehicles if you eventually plan to purchase a trailer in which to haul your machines. Most of them have enough space to hold a small vendor or two, if necessary. Most six-cylinder models will provide gas mileage in the neighborhood of 17 miles per gallon in combined city and highway driving.

Minivans and full-size cargo vans are easily configured for shelving, but you will find it easier to arrange everything within reach of either the rear or side doors, since the lack of headroom, with the addition of shelves, will force you into a constant kneeling or crouching position. The primary advantage of a minivan over a cargo van is fuel economy; many even come standard with four-cylinder engines and average about 23 miles to the gallon for combined city and highway driving.

Step vans and box trucks

A step van offers a more efficient, but more costly, transportation alternative to servicing a vending route. Similar to the larger postal service vehicles, step vans make life much easier for vending operators by providing interior standing room and loads of storage space. Most operators start with cargo vans and switch to a step van after their business has grown substantially. The money spent on one of these more expensive vehicles could be offset by less wear and tear on your back because they do not require the constant kneeling and bending needed to work out of a traditional cargo van. The tall ceiling and interior walkway make filling orders a breeze. They are also big enough to eventually incorporate a refrigerated compartment if necessary and carry full-size vendors. If you plan on hauling vendors, install a ramp or a hydraulic lift, since these vehicles are usually set higher off the ground than a van. The reduced gas mileage must also be taken into consideration when pondering this type of vehicle. A gasoline-powered step van with a 10,000-pound gross vehicle weight averages about 10 miles to the gallon, while a diesel-powered one gets about 14 miles to the gallon.

A box truck, similar to those available for rent for self-moving chores, is another option for your vending business, although the larger engines and increased vehicle height tend to reduce fuel mileage even more. But, this type of vehicle offers greater storage capacity and the ease of installing an optional lift gate for raising and lowering heavy vendors. Fuel mileage in box trucks will vary according to the size of the truck; a 26-foot model will average about seven miles to the gallon, while the smaller 10-foot box truck averages about 12 miles per gallon. Both step vans and box trucks are perfect solutions to vending operators who want to use their service vehicles for storing a large portion of their merchandise at any given time.

Next, you will need to decide whether to buy new or used. A new cargo van will run approximately $21,000 — depending on options — while a new step van or box truck could easily be double or triple that amount. Good used cargo and step vans can be found from about $10,000, while a recent model box truck might set you back close to $40,000. One good source for the latter would be self-moving rental companies, such as U-Haul International Inc. or Ryder Systems Inc. These firms have a reputation for maintaining their vehicles, and they frequently sell trucks after reaching a certain mileage point. Many of the larger box trucks they use also feature hydraulic lifts. You can check the phone book for local offices of either company or conduct an Internet search for their used vehicles.

If your budget does not allow for a new cargo van, and you do not want the expense of a step van or box truck, you can still find or create your own vending service vehicle. If you already own a pickup truck, check out the classified ads or search the Internet for used camper shells in your area. Many of these offer the standing room of a step van and could be modified to carry merchandise. This would enable you to replace just the pickup truck, if necessary, but keep the same camper shell that you have already outfitted for your business. A pickup camper would also offer you better gas mileage than either of the larger box trucks and step vans. Another option would be to buy a used airport shuttle-type van, such as those used for the Super Shuttle Company. Although these vans have windows, which makes your stock more visible to passers-by, they also have extended tops, allowing plenty of room for merchandise and for passengers to freely walk about the interior. They can easily be converted into a vending-service vehicle with shelving. Most of these also have rear air conditioning vents, so you can keep your perishables and other stock cool, even in the summer.

When comparing vehicles, new or used, get quotes from several dealers and manufacturers. Check the Internet, too. You can frequently find the same vehicle online for less, and then use that information as a bargaining tool to help obtain a better purchase price. If you decide to settle on a used vehicle, have it checked out by a reliable mechanic before you sign on the dotted line. A thorough examination can help you avoid serious underlying mechanical issues, provide you more peace of mind, and possibly give you more negotiating leverage before you close the deal.

Outfitting Your Service Vehicle

Once you have made a decision and purchased the vehicle to use in your vending business, remodel it to fit your specific needs and outfit it with all the necessary equipment and supplies. Before you decide to purchase a used vehicle, see if you can take it in for a complete service check. Have your mechanic check the spark plugs and wires and ensure that all water hoses and fan belts are in good working order. It would be a good idea to change the oil and transmission fluid, as well as do a complete radiator flush if you cannot verify that any of these have been done recently. The tires should also be checked for sufficient tread and tire pressure.

If the vehicle was not previously used to haul merchandise, install shelving and dividers, if feasible, and hire a carpenter to do so if you do not know how to do so yourself. Or, if you feel confident in your own building abilities, check at your local home improvement store, such as The Home Depot or Lowe's. They offer DIY shelving systems that might be a more affordable option. If you are going to be handling chocolates and other perishables, now is the time to permanently install a large icebox or refrigeration unit if you are working out of a large step van or box truck. If you are using a van for your service vehicle, purchase a large, sturdy ice chest, preferably with wheels, which can serve double-duty for product storage and transportation.

Permanently mount a fire extinguisher or two in your vehicle. If the driver's compartment is separate from the merchandise area, you will want at least two in your truck, one for up front and one for the merchandise area. Heavy-duty door locks should also be installed at this time, as well as any other security features, such as an alarm or backup alert.

Vehicle Outfitting Checklist

- Strong box or safe (bolted securely to the floor)
- Fire extinguisher(s)
- Large ice chest, preferably with wheels
- Dolly or other type of hand truck
- Small, handheld ice chest
- Vending machine tool box (for making minor repairs and adjustments)
- Zippered cash pouches for carrying vending machine cash

- Supply of extra security locks for vending machines

- Heavy-duty extension cords (for hooking up new vendors)

- Tape measure (for measuring entryways and distances for installing new vendors)

- Heavy-duty flashlight(s) and extra batteries

- All-purpose spray cleaner for wiping down vendors

- WD-40 or other lubricant

- Box cutter or other cutting instrument

- Clipboard or other device for holding route cards

- First-aid kit

- Sturdy cleaning rags or supply of paper towels

- Backpack or small rolling carry-on suitcase for tools and cleaning supplies

- Electrical and duct tapes

- Plastic garbage bags

Chapter Takeaways

All roads have been leading up to this event: the time when you stock your machines with a variety of products. This chapter recommends you work with product distributors, a planogram, par numbers, and membership clubs to effectively manage your product stock. You have also been challenged to consider how you will manage your seasonal stock to avoid meltdowns, spoilage, and expiration dates. Here are a few things to remember before going on to the next chapter:

- Businesses should divide products into three distinct categories: core, cycle, and choice

- Modern vending machines are now using telemetry, a wireless Internet connection that notifies vending operators when a machine is running low or is out of a particular product

- Wholesale distributors will be your most dependable source for the largest variety of products

- Before ordering merchandise for your vendors, decide how you are going to store the products so you will have a place to receive them when they are delivered

- As in any other product business, the objective in vending is to sell what you buy

- If you are going to be a snack vendor, find ways to help your products stay fresh and protected from spoilage as long as possible

- Now that you have decided what you are going to vend, decide what kind of vehicle will work for your business

- No matter which vehicle you settle on, outfit it with a safe or strong box bolted to the floor to protect the cash profits you collect daily from your vending operation

CHAPTER 10

Growing Wisely

Starting any new business can be difficult, especially if you are launching into unknown territory for the first time. What any new vending business owner needs is advice or counsel from those who have already traveled down a similar road. The tricky part is finding other vendors who will talk to you and tell you about their own successes and failures. Your best bet would not be to call established vending companies in your city or region that might view you as a potential competitor. In that case, any advice you receive might be purposely aimed at clipping the wings of your new company before it even gets off the ground. Instead, look for vendors located a considerable distance away from your region, preferably in another state. This is where the Internet can be a marvelous resource of information; you can search online to find vending operators, distributors, and vending machine manufacturers.

Use caution with some of your search results, however. Blue-sky operators will pop up frequently in your search results. Novice vending operators could easily fall prey to slick sales pitches and end up with a bunch of costly vendors and underperforming locations. Seasoned vending operators who have their own Web sites frequently offer advice or books they have written on how to succeed and avoid the pitfalls that are common to the industry. Charles Taylor of Vending Rules has written several downloadable e-books and offers vending consultations by telephone for a fee. Toronto Vending Services owner Chris Robertson has also written an e-book, containing perspective gleaned from his nine years in the industry, and promotes it via a special Web site, **www.myvendingsecret.com**. There is even a retired vending operator, Rob Farnham — on the Internet known as "My Vending Uncle" — who has written a book about how he succeeded in the industry after getting burned by a blue-sky scammer. You can also read comments from vending operators and post questions on vending blogs, which you can find by simply using a search engine.

The Vending Yellow Pages Directory, part of the **www.vending-connection.com**, is a terrific resource for finding other vending operators and just about any kind of information you desire on the vending industry. Here, you can find lists of vending machine manufacturers and distributors, product distributors, locating and repair services, and much more. If you do not have Internet access at home, most local libraries have computers to use for free, and you normally do not have to have a library card. If visiting the library is not feasible, check the classified section of several out-of-town newspapers to see if any vendors are advertising in them. You might even call local vendors and ask if they know of any in another region, pretending to be an interested location manager.

Plug In to Your New Industry

One of the best ways to get informed about the vending industry and its new trends is through professional trade organizations and publications. Common vending organizations include:

- **The National Automatic Merchandising Association (NAMA)**: The national trade association of the food and refreshment vending, coffee services, and food service management. Since 1936, this association has been driven by its mission to collectively advance and promote the automatic merchandising and coffee industries.

- **The National Bulk Vendors Association (NBVA)**: Representing the bulk vending industry since 1950, the NBVA is a nonprofit trade association made up of distributors, manufacturers, and operators of bulk vending machines and products.

The vending industry organizations usually hold trade shows once or twice a year, which offer a platform for all the different players to come together, including manufacturers, distributors, locating companies, and others. Once you start studying a particular organization and reading its publications, you might decide to become a member. Many of these trade organizations produce their own publications, offer various products and services, and sponsor one or more shows annually. Being a member could prove to be a most advantageous wealth of information. Most of the annual membership fees cost more than $200, but you can always attend the trade shows and simply pay a slightly higher nonmember price with no other obligation. Attending trade shows gives you the advantage of networking with other vending operators from across the country. It is an easy environment in which to relax, make new acquaintances, and learn from one another's mistakes and successes as you gather new ideas for your business.

Trade publications are good sources for learning about the latest vendors, merchandise, even service vehicles. The classified advertising sections are good places to shop for used vendors and other equipment. You can also check out the online versions of the trade publications, such as *Automatic Merchandiser* (**www.amonline.com**) and *Vending Times* (**www.vendingtimes.com**), which allow you to access current and archived news articles, browse the classified advertising, and view Web casts and blogs.

Stay Small or Grow Big?

After you have been at your vending business for a good while, you will have learned how to effectively manage your merchandise flow, the trick of properly timing your service calls, and how to deal effectively with location managers. You might have even become so successful that you have given up your day job and now have a full-time dedication to your vending operation. But what happens when you suddenly find yourself running on all eight cylinders and still do not have enough time to get everything done? You now find yourself at a crossroads: You must decide if you are satisfied with your company in its present state or want to expand even further. The former means you have reached your business potential as an independent route operator, while the latter means it is now time to seek outside help to manage the business.

Although it might be hard to pinpoint at exactly what time your business can profitably support paid employees, large operators frequently say a vending business should be bringing in at least

$5,000 a week or almost $300,000 gross a year before attempting to do so. Your personal goals and desires will determine the next step. Now might be time to pull out your mission statement and business plan to see if either needs tweaking or if you have strayed too far from the original goals. If it is time to tweak the plan, perhaps you will want to consider hiring help to service your machines.

Many successful vendors are happy to stay small and etch out a good living for themselves and their families as independent vending operators. Even if you do not want to go through the hoops of hiring employees, there are still growth opportunities for operators whose family members are willing to lend a hand. Working with family members can be easier since you do not have to put children on payroll and your spouse can be considered part of the sole proprietorship. A lot of vending companies are run by couples that divide up the chores and even service separate routes. If your spouse has been working outside of the home but has been watching from the sidelines as you have grown your business, perhaps now is the time to recruit him or her into the business. Your older children can also help out, since many routes can be serviced in the evenings and on the weekends. If you are going to use your children (between the ages of 10 and 17), however, you must train them adequately, especially in the area of safety precautions. Since vending is an all-cash business, they must be taught how to safeguard themselves and the proceeds. Remind them that they are to always park the service vehicle in a well-lit and highly visible spot as close to the service doors as possible. They should also be trained to keep an eye out for any suspicious behavior and notify you by cell phone at once if they have the slightest doubt about a person or situation.

Try to avoid having them work much after dark, and if any of your vendors are located in questionable locations, it would be best to service those yourself. If possible, pay your older children the same as you would pay anyone else their age for working. In this way, they will reap the benefits of participating in the family business. Younger children, ages 8 to 12, can also be drafted to help unpack and sort merchandise deliveries, load the service vehicles, and ride along with you to help service the machines when they are not in school. By compensating them for their time with special perks or treats, such as money for an ice cream cone while working, video rentals, and even an unexpected gift now and then, you will also make them feel like a part of the family business and its rewards.

If you do not have the option of recruiting a spouse or children, the next best option is to recruit other family members or trustworthy friends. These will have to be compensated on a more official level than immediate family members, since they will be working for your business. Because you will most likely only need someone part-time at the start, it is best to consider those who are already working, but who are in need of extra income. Start by paying them a nominal fee to ride along with you one day as you service the route. That way, you can allow them to watch you restock vendors, remove the cash, and fill out the route cards, as well as try their hand at it themselves. You will know at the end of the route if he or she is a good candidate or not.

College students and retired individuals (between the ages of 55 and 70) are also good part-time help possibilities because they are usually in need of extra income. If you are unsure where to look, contact the student employment office of your local university or visit the office of a nearby retirement community. The clubhouses in retirement communities often have bulletin boards where you can place an announcement without cost.

Another possible source for employees is the U.S. Government's Welfare-to-Work program as part of the U.S. Office for Personnel Management (**www.opm.gov/wtw**). This program pays employers to train workers, as well as paying the workers while they undergo training, a service that can provide significant savings to your company. The only stipulation is that you must guarantee the trained employee a job for at least a year and provide him or her with health benefits. A simple search on the Internet will provide you with numerous companies offering such benefits. All it takes is a few e-mails or phone calls to get comparison quotes.

Hiring from the general public

When hiring strangers, it is best to go through the official application and interview process. You can easily find standard employment applications at most office supply stores, and once the prospective employee fills it out, tell him or her that you will call within the next day or two to let him or her know your decision. This will give you time to call the candidate's former places of employment and verify the reasons for leaving. Although a former employer is legally bound from negatively describing a former employee, the company can tell you if the person left voluntarily or was let go. You should ask for at least two or three personal references and call them, too. Finally, you should also rely on your own intuition with making an employment decision. If you feel good about an individual and your personalities click, that might be all you need. Even so, you should still perform a background check on any person you are seriously considering for employment. You will find various online businesses dedicated to conducting these for a fee ranging from $25 to $160, which includes CriminalData.com (**www.criminaldata.com**) and easyBackgrounds (**www.easybackgrounds.com**), among others.

Because any employee could essentially be dealing with the cash proceeds of your business, you must feel that you are able to trust him or her. By this stage of the game, you should already have a general idea of the money made on particular routes and from individual locations, and you should share this information with your new employee. That way he or she will know that you would automatically notice any significant deviations. If you train him or her to always fill out the route reports with the amount removed from each machine, it will help reinforce the idea. By counting the money at that time, you will notice if something is amiss after he or she turns in the route cards. You should also make it a point to understand your employee's financial situation at home. If you suspect your profits are being skimmed by an employee, it is best to confront him or her and risk hurt feelings than to let it continue unabated, which will cost you more in the long run. If it is still going on after the confrontation, you should let that employee go and look for more trustworthy help.

Employees should also be trained to take the same safety precautions you yourself take when servicing machines. Teach them to always wait until the last minute before leaving a location to remove the money from the vending machines, as well as safeguarding the bank bags until the money is securely deposited in the service vehicle's safe. Never share the safe combination with your employees; that way, they will have a defense if ever faced with an attempted robbery. Warn them to always comply with a would-be robber and hand over the bank bag if asked to do so.

You can frequently find vending employee training tips in industry publications and some of the major snack food distributors provide training resources for improving product sales.

Keeping Your Employees and Company Safe

Once you become an employer, a first step should be to compile an employee handbook or manual. You might think that as a small company you would rather not be so formal, and instead prefer to treat your employees more like family. Keeping everything — even the basic rules of conduct — on such an informal level could end up costing you in the long run. For example, if you send out a new employee in a work vehicle, but do not stipulate in writing that he or she cannot drink while on the job, you as the business owner could be liable in court for any damages he or she causes in an accident. Just as with large businesses, small companies can be subject to sexual harassment suits and other litigation, so your first line of defense is to have your company's policies in writing. You will want to consider subjects such as employee conduct, dress code, evaluations, employee harassment, company holidays, employee leaves, insurance, security issues, smoking policy, company vehicles, and computer equipment. *A sample employee handbook is available on the companion CD-ROM.* Most companies also require the employee to sign a document stating that he or she has received a copy of the handbook, which further relieves the employer of being accused in court of not informing an employee of his or her official duties and responsibilities.

Although you can put together a simple employee handbook yourself, you would be wise to seek outside legal counsel on the finished project to ensure you have covered all of the necessary topics. A basic employee manual should include, but not be limited, to the following topics: your company's mission statement and purpose, employee responsibilities and duties, work hours and expectations for workplace behavior, safety and health policies and procedures, vacation days and sick leave — if any — and who to contact to arrange these, medical insurance and retirement benefits, your firm's sexual harassment and discrimination policies, procedures for resolving grievances, and resignation and termination policies.

You can find advice and commentary online about putting together an employee handbook, as well as templates for sale that you can adapt and personalize to the needs of your own company. Most of these will run you about $100 and can include state-specific compliance language. Compare several of these before making a decision, since they offer different services, templates, and topics. *See Appendix B for a list of such templates.*

Adhering to OSHA standards

Even if you only plan on having one employee, your company will still be subject to Occupational Safety and Health Administration (OSHA) regulations. To avoid workman's compensation claims and employee downtime due to on-the-job injuries, you must meticulously teach every employee how to properly lift heavy boxes and loads. If you have computer access, you will find the OSHA Web site (**www.osha.gov**) to be a valuable resource in safety and compliance information, training materials, news, and more. Be sure to place OSHA safety instructional brochures or posters in a prominent place, such as a break room or inside the service vehicles. These are available without cost on the organization's Web site, or you can order them by telephone at (202) 693-1888.

Your employees should be taught how to correctly operate any heavy equipment, such as a forklift or hand truck, and to use extreme caution when moving and transporting heavy vending machines. The OSHA Web site also offers a special section for small business information. Another helpful Web site for employee safety includes the United States Department of Labor (**www.dol.gov**), which provides a lot of useful information on workers' compensation issues and workplace safety and health.

It is crucial for your employees to understand they will be representing you when out in the field servicing the routes. You can never overemphasize courtesy and respect when teaching them how to relate to your location managers, especially in the area of refunds, vendor repairs, and any other customer service issues. Without this proper training, your new employees could easily undo what has taken you years of good interpersonal skills to create.

Programs such as Payroll Mate (**www.realtaxtools.com**) are available for less than $100 and automatically calculate federal withholding, social security, and Medicaid taxes, in addition to printing checks and maintaining archives of all past payroll periods. QuickBooks (**http://quickbooks.intuit.com**) offers similar software to Peachtree® or Microsoft® Office Accounting, as well as additional payroll tax services. If you do not want to do it yourself, there are a variety of online services, such as PayCycle (**www.paycycle.com**), which charge reasonable monthly rates and even offer 30-day free trials.

Paying Wages and Benefits

If you are a small vending company about to hire your first employee, you will probably be inclined to only pay minimum wage and not offer any other benefits. You are the one who ultimately will decide what to offer, but you must realize that minimum wage pay can attract employees that are looking for something more part-time and is usually best reserved for part-time workers who have other income sources. At that salary level, you will also be competing with a host of other businesses whose work might not be so labor intensive as a vending route. Employees will sometimes jump ship for the same pay, but much easier work or hours. For an idea of what the pay norm is for vending route drivers and other industry workers, you can purchase a copy of the biannual "Wage, Rates, and Benefits Survey" conducted by the National Automatic Merchandising Association; however, at $200, you might be better off using that money to pay a better salary to begin with.

If you have never had an employee before, you must face the realization that it will be your responsibility to pay this person during the good and bad times. You might have been willing to go without any compensation while your business was growing, but an employee will never have the same kind of loyalty as the owner. You need to face the possibility of having to pay your employee or employees when your business is temporarily in the red and the money is not there for their salaries. Before you hire your first part-time employee, you should begin to put aside a regular amount of money into an emergency fund so you will have enough money to make payroll, even in the bad times.

Although costly, benefits are another popular way to attract and keep good employees. You may not be able to offer medical insurance and sick pay in the beginning, but you should at least offer your full-time employees a week of paid vacation the first year and increase it to two weeks after the second year of employment. Lower-paid employees tend to have fewer resources for unexpected medical emergencies than higher-paid ones, so you should attempt to add medical as soon as you are financially able. Until you offer medical insurance, you can do what some other vending operators have done in the interim, which is offer to pay the employee's treatments at a local urgent care center. This is an excellent alternative to medical insurance and, once you fill out the paperwork, the clinic might even bill you directly rather than bill your employee.

Businesses that eventually grow enough to have one or more employees need to consider the possibility of offering a retirement plan to help retain good workers. Two of the simplest types of these for small businesses are a payroll deduction individual retirement account (IRA) and a Savings Incentive Match Plan for Employees (SIMPLE). For the former, all you need do is arrange a payroll deduction plan for an IRA with your financial institution or insurance firm. Your employees decide if they want to participate and how much to have deducted every pay period. You could also offer them the choice of a traditional IRA, whose savings grow tax-deferred until withdrawal, or a Roth IRA, which uses after-tax contributions. Neither of these require much paperwork or a financial commitment on the part of the employer.

On the other hand, a SIMPLE retirement plan requires the employer to match the dollar amount of each employee's contributions up to 3 percent of his or her pay. A SIMPLE plan can be set up as a 401(k) or a Roth IRA account. Since this will cost you more, you might only want to consider implementing this type of plan if you are concerned about good employees jumping ship for better benefits elsewhere.

If you would rather leave all of this planning to someone else, one of the easiest ways to open up a series of excellent benefits for your employees is by obtaining membership for your company in a local credit union. Your vending company's membership in a credit union will open up a slew of new services for yourself and your employees, including checking accounts, certificates of deposit and IRAs, a variety of loan programs, and open lines of credit. Most credit unions will charge you nothing as an employer to join, but not all of them accept new members. The Web site of the National Credit Union Administration will be your best place to begin your search (**www.ncua.gov**).

As an employer, you can also arrange for a series of perks for your employees that will not necessarily hit you hard in the pocketbook. You can be as creative as you want in developing perks, which can include such benefits as reduced membership fees in warehouse club-type stores, like Costco and Sam's Club, where you are a corporate member; discounts to movie theaters or area attractions; or reduced cost or supplemental insurance plans that can be payroll deducted.

Payroll Taxes

Paying payroll taxes is a somewhat complicated issue you will need to tackle if you plan on having employees. Although you can hire out your payroll duties to various services, you might not be willing or able to pay for it in the beginning. It is best to at least learn the basics of what your payroll responsibilities are so you can correctly perform these duties. Your first step will be to obtain an Employer Identification Number (EIN) if you are not already operating a sole proprietorship under one. You can get one by providing the necessary information for IRS form SS-4 over the phone to an IRS representative (800-829-4933) or download the form from the IRS Web site (go to **www.irs.gov** and click on the link for "more forms and publications"). You must also make sure your bank accepts federal tax deposits — or find one that does — and obtain a federal tax deposit coupon book, which can be requested over the phone. Your first coupon will come with your EIN package. Any employee you hire must also fill out a W-4 form, which you can also download from the IRS Web site, as well as a state-withholding certificate if your particular state has an income tax. You will need to consult your state department of revenue to obtain the form, as well as to find out how and when you need to deposit your employee's state income taxes.

The three main payroll taxes you must be concerned with are the income taxes you withhold from an employee's earnings (federal and state, if applicable), Medicare and social security (that you and the employee pay half), and unemployment, which you, as the employer, pay all. Medicare and social security, which are also known as Federal Insurance Contributions Act (FICA) taxes, are less complicated because they are strictly federal taxes, while unemployment must be dealt with on both the state and federal levels and requires keeping stricter records.

Federal income taxes deducted from an employee's paycheck are figured by following the methods detailed in the Employer's Tax Guide (IRS Publications 15), coupled with withholding information from the particular employee's form W-4. The FICA taxes are fairly easy to compute, consisting of a 6.2 percent social security tax and a Medicare tax of 1.4 percent. Simply multiply the employee's gross wages by the particular percentage to get the tax amount. You, as the employer, must match the exact same amount.

You must also pay federal unemployment taxes, also known as Federal Unemployment Tax Act (FUTA). This tax is used for payments of unemployment compensation to workers who have lost their jobs. The FUTA gross tax rate of 6.2 percent only applies to the first $7,000 earned annually by an employee, and the federal government provides up to a 5.4 percent tax credit for the state unemployment tax (State Unemployment Tax Act, or SUTA) you pay. The SUTA tax can go up or down, depending on how many recent unemployment claims have been filed against your company. For whatever percentage it goes up, your FUTA tax goes down. For example, if your state unemployment tax is 2.2 percent, then you will actually also pay 4 percent in federal unemployment taxes for a total of 6.2 percent. If your SUTA tax goes up 1 percent to 3.2 percent, then you only pay 3 percent in FUTA tax.

All payroll taxes you deduct from your employees' paychecks must be turned in to the IRS by a certain date each week or month, or your business will be hit with late fees and interest. The size of your payroll will dictate how often you must deposit your federal payroll taxes. Since you are contemplating your first employees, you will most likely be depositing on a monthly basis, usually by the 15th of each calendar month. Only businesses whose previous year's federal tax deposits exceeded $50,000 must make biweekly deposits. You must ensure you make your federal tax deposits by the end of your bank's particular working day on the 15th, which can be as early as 2 p.m. Otherwise, your business will be subject to penalties and interest. For example, a failure-to-file fine is calculated based on the time from the deadline of your tax return, extensions included, to the date you actually filed your tax return There is a special holiday rule that makes an exception for when the 15th falls on a weekend or bank holiday. Your deposit is then due on the next official business banking day. You can also sign up to pay your federal tax deposits by automatic wire transfer via the Electronic Federal Tax Payment System. Simply visit the Web site at **www.eftps.gov** for more information.

As an employer, you will be obligated to file a quarterly report known as the Employer's Quarterly Federal Tax Return, Form 941, by the last day of the month following the end of each quarter. This form is used to total up the federal taxes you owe and compare that to what you paid through the quarter. If you have not yet paid your employer-matching FICA funds for social security and Medicare or owe any federal unemployment taxes, you will need to enclose a check for the difference along with the report. By January 31 of every year you had an employee the previous year, you must also fill out and submit the Employer's Annual Federal Unemployment Tax Return, Form 940. There is a simpler version of the form for smaller employers, known as Form 940-EZ. You will find these and all other necessary payroll tax forms on the IRS Web site, along with instructional booklets and plenty of other information to help guide you through the process.

You must also send out a Wage and Tax Statement, Form W-2, by January 31 to everyone you employed during the previous year, which details exactly how much they paid in income taxes and how much you paid in FICA and unemployment taxes. These forms are necessary for them to file their individual tax returns, and you must also send a copy to the Social Security Administration.

Is It Time to Take on a Partner?

Of course, another option to hiring employees is to take on a partner in your vending business. Opening up your established company to a partner in lieu of hiring someone opens up the door to an infusion of new capital and avoids the headache of dealing with payroll taxes. Instead of paying your new associate a salary, you can offer a percentage of the business in exchange for a financial investment. The percentage amount would depend on the investment amount. If your prospective partner is willing and able to invest the same amount you did originally to launch your business, you could offer to divide the profits 50-50. If the investment is less, you could offer the same profit percentage comparable to the investment percentage or whatever number you mutually agree on.

Whatever terms you decided upon for your business, these need to be drawn up legally through the use of a partnership agreement, which should also state how to address grievances and the potential dissolution of the partnership, transfer of interests, withdrawal, death or removal of a partner, capitalization, allocation of profits and losses, and miscellaneous items. There are also other legal requirements, such as annually filing the IRS Form 1065, which details the current condition of your business and partnership. Your new partner's income taxes will be treated just as your own, filed in a pass-through taxation (the partnership is not directly taxed; the tax burden is instead passed on to the partners) format via Form 1040.

You should think long and hard before you choose someone to be your business partner. You probably have invested a significant portion of your life and finances to getting your business where it is today, and you do not want to risk your hard-earned success by partnering with the wrong person. This decision should not be based solely on financial capability, but also on the prospective partner's business sense, personality, and past endeavors. You need to be just as diligent in choosing a partner as you would be in hiring an employee. A prospective partner should provide you with business and personal references, as well as current financial data to back up his or her ability to make an investment in your company. This will require diligence and hard work on your part to follow through and make the necessary contacts, as well as perform a background check on him or her. This might be a lot of work, but it is better than taking a risk with the good reputation of your vending business.

Naming your partnership

If you have been operating your vending business under your own name, you will need to choose another name to represent the combined business efforts of you and your new partner. When deciding on a company name, you must ensure that the name has not already been trademarked (for more information on trademark infringement, refer back to Chapter 2). One way to avoid any legal entanglements with a name is to simply create a fusion between your name and that of your prospective partner. It could be a combination of either your first name or his or her last name, or actually fusing your two first or last names (for example Smith and Williams Vending, John Jacob Vendors, etc.). You should also stipulate this name in the partnership agreement, along with who will retain the rights to it if the partnership eventually dissolves. As with the actual terms of the partnership, this must be resolved early on, since it could force you to change the company name again if you part ways.

Getting Additional Help

Launching your own vending business might seem to be a daunting task at times, but do not go it completely alone. There is a world of available resources at your fingertips, thanks to organizations such as the U.S. Small Business Administration (**www. sba.gov**). The SBA was founded in 1953 with the goal of helping Americans "start, build, and grow businesses," and today offers a wealth of tools to entrepreneurs like yourself.

The SBA's Web site provides information on everything from finding a business mentor to choosing your business structure, obtaining financing, and fulfilling all necessary licensing requirements. There are links to guides for managing employees, paying taxes, and handling all of the legal aspects of starting a new company. You can also find information on SBA loans and grants, advice on bidding for government contracts, and links to free online courses. In addition to the information this book has provided you for managing employees, the SBA Web site offers supplemental information that would be a helpful resource.

You might also find help from a business incubator located in your own community. Frequently located on college campuses, these are organizations that provide office space, machinery, and other resources at sharply reduced rates for new businesses trying to get off the ground. The National Business Incubation Association (**www.nbia.org**) offers information and links to the business incubators in every state. A business mentor can help you get started down the right path by offering advice from personal experience. SCORE "Counselors to America's Small Businesses" (**www.score.org**) is a non-profit resource partner of SBA and offers free face-to-face and online business counseling, as well as online workshops. More than 10,000 working and retired business owners and executives from across the nation donate their time as SCORE volunteers to help entrepreneurs start new businesses.

Your own community most likely has a variety of business development resources available for you. Check the phone book or search online for business or economic development organizations in your hometown. Representatives from these entities will know if there are any local government incentives for which you could apply, and could direct you down the right path for business incubators and even loans or grants for minority- or women-owned businesses.

Chris Robertson said that already-established vending operators could be a good source of information, if you can get beyond the wall they sometimes put up for fear of competition. "In this business, everyone puts too much emphasis on competition," he said. "They don't want to help anyone else just starting out. Some guys will give you the cold shoulder, but others won't."

There are numerous online resources for information on new business startup, as well. Web sites such as **www.startupnation. com** and **www.entrepreneur.com** are great for advice on business planning and how to launch your company's Web site. The Internet is also full of blogs, such as **www.howtobesuccessfulinthevendingbusiness.blogspot.com**, where vending operators share their successes and failures with the rest of the world.

Many successful vending operators have also written books on their experiences to help others avoid the mistakes and pitfalls new operators frequently make. You will find personal experiences from vending professionals, such as Rob Farnham (**www.my-vending-uncle.com**), Chris Robertson (**www.myvendingsecret.com**), Ronnie Talent (**www.vendingjackpot.com**), Charles Taylor (**www.vendingrules.com**), and Bill Way (**www.livefree.com**) throughout this book. All of these operators-turned-authors share their own trials and errors and warn entrepreneurs to avoid the costly mistake of getting entangled with blue-sky vending scams. Robertson's and Taylor's books are presently only available in electronic versions via Web site download, but both offer additional forms of vending business counseling. Rob Farnham, Chris Robertson, and Ronnie Talent invite those who register on their Internet sites to participate in Web-based telephone training calls, while Taylor offers telephone consultations by the half-hour or hour to help new vendors find firm footing in the vending industry.

Chapter Takeaways

A quick and painful way to fail in business is to try to go it alone. All successful business owners have had help along the way, even if they started out as a sole proprietor. When it comes to addressing issues like learning a new industry, staying small versus growing big, managing employees, or taking on a partner, it is important to seek extra help from more knowledgeable sources. Use the Internet as a primary resource to find additional help, but do not forget your local community, as well. Before you decide to grow your business, consider these few points:

- What any new vending business owner needs is advice or counsel from those who have already traveled a similar road

- One of the best ways to inform yourself about the vending industry and its new trends is through professional trade organizations and publications

- Look to family members, trustworthy friends, college students, and retired individuals for help with your growing business

- If you decide to become an employer, one of your first steps should be to compile an employee handbook or manual

- Whether you have one employee or 50, your company will be subject to OSHA regulations

- It is crucial when training your employees that they understand they will be representing you when out in the field servicing the routes

- Another option to hiring employees is to take on a partner in your vending business

- Launching your own vending business might seem to be a daunting task at times, but do not go it alone

CHAPTER 11

Off-road Requirements

O nce you have restocked and dusted off your last vendor, dumped the proceeds in your cash box, and headed your service vehicle toward home, it might be tempting to focus on the recliner, television, and remote control. Unfortunately, that inclination is premature. As the owner of your own vending company, there is still plenty of work to do before calling it a night. One of the most important daily chores you will perform is preparing your bank deposit.

Taking It to the Bank

Since vending proceeds consist of change and small denomination bills, sort and roll the coins and band or package the currency. If you are just starting out in your vending business, you will most likely be sorting and rolling your change by hand, with the help of a set of plastic coin counters. Once your business grows substantially, make use of machines that can count change electronically.

One option is to take the change to self-service coin counters, which are available at supermarkets and other locations.

Although these might take a lot of hassle out of the job, you can pay as much 10 percent of the counted money for the service and you will still have to take the money to the bank. Some of these coin machines do count change for free if converted into gift cards for area businesses or services, but you will not always find those to be helpful when you want to pay bills. Instead, shop around for a bank that offers free self-service coin counters in its branch lobbies and switch your commercial account to one of its branches. The savings in time and added convenience would make the switch well worth it. For a state-by-state listing of banks and other locations with free or inexpensive coin-counting services, visit the Coin Counting Web site at **www.the-understory.com** and click on your home state.

Another option would be to purchase your own coin-counting machine for your office. Through a simple Internet search, you can find digital coin-counting machines beginning around $50; currency counters start around $200. *For other supplies, see Appendix B.*

Once the bills and coins are counted and wrapped, it is time to make your bank deposit. With most commercial bank accounts you will receive a deposit book where you detail all your cash, coin, and check deposits. Although you do not need to be concerned with checks for a vending business, you will want to carefully total up your cash, fill in the appropriate spaces on the deposit slip, and recheck your figures. If you use a bank with a free coin-counting service, you might not have the luxury of a large adding machine. You will have to rely on the small digital version available at most financial institutions' lobby kiosks. This will require even more meticulous rechecking of your calculations to ensure that there are no errors when you reach the teller window.

Decide what time of day is best to make deposits. Since you still have to wrap and roll your proceeds once you get home, it might be best to go to the bank first thing in the morning before you begin route maintenance. If you must begin your route before banking hours, securely lock your deposit in your vehicle's strongbox until you get a chance to make a deposit later in the day. Try varying your route to your local bank branch or visit a different branch each day you make your deposit. Another security practice is to vary the time of day you make your deposits. Both of these practices will make it more difficult for someone to follow you, thereby decreasing your chances of a break-in.

Reloading and Restocking Your Service Vehicle

At the end of the day, replenish your service vehicle with enough stock for the next day. Whether you perform this duty at the end of the day or in the morning before you begin your route depends on what time of the day you arrive home and how early you begin the next day's route. If you have early and late locations on the same day, it might be more feasible to return to your home or warehouse over the lunch hour for restocking.

If possible, this is a chore that can be tasked to older children after school for monetary or other compensation. It is also a great way to keep them interested in the business. If you do not have children, find a neighborhood high school or college student who would be willing to help out a few hours a week for extra income. Either way, train stock helpers exactly how you want your service vehicle loaded and which products in what quantities must be on board. They must also understand your route schedule to know which routes consist of bulk vendors and which ones consist of snack and beverage vendors.

Any damaged or returned items must be placed in the proper receptacles. When restocking your vehicle, you or your helpers must document the total merchandise on hand in your warehouse or storage building. This is where the par merchandising system that was discussed in "Managing Your Stock" section of Chapter 9 comes into play. You and any outside help you use in stock work must know the par of each item that you carry so the item can be placed on an order list as soon as its par is reached. To make this easier, the par for each individual item should be written next to the item in question, and you should keep a clipboard and writing instrument hanging on the wall in your warehouse or stockroom to access at a moment's notice. Keeping track of your par levels must become such a habit that you or your helper reach for the clipboard every time before loading the item on the service vehicle. Each day after the vehicle is restocked, take the clipboard to your office and list the items that have reached their par level on an order form.

Time for the office chair

After you have taken care of your restocking chores and completed your bank deposit, the next step is to record — either manually or into a computer software program — the data entered on the route cards. A desktop computer and a good software program are highly recommended to facilitate inventory management and help you keep track of sales trends. You will find route cards to be invaluable in tracking each location's sales from week to week or month to month. They can even help track what products sell better during certain seasons or times of the year for better vendor stocking.

After entering the information from the route cards, record the products at par from your warehouse clipboard onto order forms. You might even be able to program your vending software to notify you when you reach par on certain items with a pop-up warning or through the use of software designed to remind you of specific dates or events. By taking the information from both sources, you should be able to complete your weekly orders without overlooking anything. Be sure to schedule time during the week for ordering. There are programs that can send an e-mail reminder to your cell phone about an upcoming order deadline so you do not forget to order more stock. Set aside an entire day for office chores, or various hours throughout the week either before or after servicing your routes. Your office time during the week can also be used for cold calling or preparing and mailing flyers to potential new locations.

Do not forget to enter returned products under the "waste" category of your route cards into your software program or manual list. You must keep a running total of these amounts for entering on the profit and loss statement, or Schedule C, of your annual income tax return. Also, keep a list of products that have run low and missed the order deadline in case you need to make a quick trip to a warehouse club store for emergency supplies.

If you have employees, much of the work previously described in the "Payroll Taxes" section of Chapter 10 will be performed in the office, unless you opt to pay a payroll service. Planning and implementation of employee benefits will also be managed while in the office.

Marketing Your Business

For your business to thrive and continue growing, it is imperative to develop and implement a successful marketing campaign. Much of this can be done during office time and implemented intermittently as you service your routes. As mentioned earlier, one of the best ways to maintain your business is through a good relationship with location managers. This can be done by consistently fulfilling customer requests and customizing your vending machines to particular locations.

Attracting new customers or locations, however, requires a more focused marketing strategy and a complete understanding of the types of locations you want to add to your lineup. Once you determine who your target market is, you can begin your focused attack. There are several cost-effective tools you can use to reach your marketing goals, including business cards, flyers, brochures, and your own Web site.

The tried-and-true business card

If you have not ordered business cards yet, do so as soon as possible. You will find them to be essential in presenting yourself to new location managers and getting your name and vending company into the public eye. Since your vendors are one of your most visible selling tools, consider buying a few small plastic cardholders and attaching them to several of your vendors. Leave a few business cards in the holders and refill as needed. You never know when someone in need of vending services might be passing through one of your locations. That person might not be brave enough to ask the location manager for your name, but might grab your business card to give contact you later. Each of your vendors should also have your company name and contact information prominently displayed in an eye-level location, if possible. If not, leave a business card or two on bulletin boards in your present locations or other public areas with a lot of foot traffic.

Business cards are also useful for sending out query letters to prospective locations. A location manager might pitch the letter after reading it, but a card will most likely go into a Rolodex for later reference. A week or two later, follow up each location query letter with a telephone call to confirm receipt and reinforce your marketing message. If you are unsure how to put together a convincing query letter, use the sample that follows (also on the accompanying CD). Simply insert your own name, title, company name, and the name of the location manager. Now you are ready to make contact.

Social networking

The most traditional form of social networking is to join your local Chamber of Commerce to see if you can join a few of the networking events they host monthly. If you want to be more tech-savvy about your social networking, try any or all of the online communities, such as Facebook (**www.facebook.com**), Twitter (**www.twitter.com**), or LinkedIn® (**www.linkedin.com**). These sites can be a great outlet for marketing yourself and your business, developing relationships, and exchanging ideas and information with others in your industry. Furthermore, these services are free and reach your target audience; the only thing you will have to dedicate is your time, which may be hard to come by when first starting your vending business.

Magnetic signs, brochures, and Web sites

Magnetic signs for your service vehicle are another relatively low-cost form of constant advertising exposure, starting as low as $25 per decal. These should be big enough to include your company name and phone number in large letters and numbers. Magnetic signs are a great alternative to simply painting your logo on the vehicle, because they last two to four years, are fade resistant, and are easy to install and remove. These magnetic signs can be purchased online through dealers like Magnetic Signs (**www.magneticsignsontime.com**), Build a Sign (**www.buildasign.com**), or Wholesale Magnetic Signs (**www.wholesalemagneticsigns.com**).

Brochures, if you decide to get a full-color, glossy one printed, can be a slightly more expensive method of getting your company's name and information out to perspective locations. These are usually large enough to include interesting information and facts about your company, photos of vending equipment and products, and details of your firm's services. Brochures are also useful for mailing out with query letters, but should be used on a more restricted basis due to the expense of printing them. Send brochures out to locations with which you have had previous telephone or e-mail communications, or drop them off personally to locations of particular interest.

Web sites are becoming a more important marketing tool day by day. Only a few decades ago, people searching for information reached for the Yellow Pages. Now, they reach for a mouse and keyboard on their way to their destination. Modern business owners understand this trend and are making Web site development and hosting part of their marketing strategy. It would be wise to do the same, because a Web site can provide a lot of publicity for a low monthly cost. It is also effective for closing the sale without a lot of follow-up effort. By incorporating colorful photos of your vendors and merchandise with pertinent information about your vending company, you give readers (and potential customers) all the information they need to make a knowledgeable vending decision. By the time they pick up the phone to call you, they already know about your company and are seriously considering your services.

Chris Robertson of Toronto Vending Services said he gets most of his new business referrals through his Web site, which has become his primary marketing tool. "My inbox is full," he said. "I get all kinds of e-mails looking for information on my business. Everything now either comes from people coming to my Web site, or they may have seen my name from an article online that I have written."

There are a number of online services offering "free" Web site building that you can do yourself, such as Website Builder (**www. sitecube.com**) and Homestead (**www.homestead.com**), which offer free trials (10 days and 30 days, respectively), but charge a low monthly hosting fee of about $5 after that. These are fine to begin with if you are working with limited funds, but eventually you will be better off paying someone to professionally design your Web site, as well as host the site. The latter is the real secret to a successful Web presence. If you have the most beautiful and innovative Web site in the world and no one is seeing it, it is all for naught. A successful Web site host will help your company's name come up in all the right Internet search strings. Top Web site hosting companies will provide:

•   Planning for search engine optimization and visibility

- A strategy for the overall marketing and structure of your Web site

- A method for keeping your Web site fresh and up-to-date

- A means for solving your customers' problems

- Usability solutions that are appropriate for your audience

Finding a good hosting company will require some research. Start online with a search for good Web hosting providers. A good rule of thumb is to follow the hosting companies that the tech companies recommend. Start with Web sites such as FindMyHosting.com (**www.findmyhosting.com**) and Web Hosting Search (**www.webhostingsearch.com**) to find a review and comparisons of some of the top Web hosting providers.

Another interesting way to get new customers is through business referrals. You could call or write all of your present location managers to introduce a new incentive program, through which you are offering cash rewards or other perks for successful location referrals. Emphasize that the incentive will only be paid upon signing a vending contract with the location he or she has referred to your business. Send business cards to all of your locations in case the managers have misplaced them.

Media marketing

Other ways to get exposure for your vending firm include radio or newspaper advertising, advertising on public buses and other transportation, and through sponsoring local sports teams (with your name clearly splashed across the jerseys or T-shirts). Robertson says the success of a vending business is almost guaranteed if the owner makes good marketing and advertising choices. "If you just take the profits and reinvest them into the marketing and advertising and buying more machines, you will make money in this business," he said. "If you spend it on beer and wings at the local bar, it will satisfy you for a couple of hours, but it won't make you any money."

Be Your Own Public Relations Firm

Most new small businesses would be hesitant to contract a public relations firm to help get their word out because of the relatively high cost; but, that should not stop you from using some of the same public relations techniques. Any good public relations representative knows the advantage of getting out and mingling with the public, a technique often referred to as networking. This is one of the least expensive forms of public relations, and it can reap great benefits and secure exposure for your business.

One way to network is to join local civic groups, such as Optimist International or Shriners International, or veterans groups such as the American Legion or Veterans of Foreign Wars. Do not be shy to talk about what you do when asked, and always carry a pocket full of business cards with you wherever you go. Your area chamber of commerce is another good source for networking, as well as other local business alliances in your area. A quick Internet search can help lead you to groups near you, and you can also look in the Yellow Pages of the phone book under "Business and Trade Organizations."

Submit a query letter

If you want to expose your business to a larger audience, one of the best ways to do that is by writing an article for a trade publication. Before you just send your article off to the magazine or trade journal, you will need to contact the editor to find out what type of submission guidelines the publication has. Most magazines and journals request that you send a query letter first outlining your topic and idea. A query letter is made of a proposed article title, the major points you intend to cover, why this information is important to the readers of the publication, and your qualifications for writing the piece.

When submitting a query letter, always enclose a standard, letter-sized, self-addressed stamped envelope. If you do not hear from the editor within six to eight weeks, feel free to follow up. Editors have a lot of query letters coming in, so give them a substantial amount of time before contacting them. If you get to the point where you have written several articles for a particular editor, he or she may not need you to submit a query letter. The editor may just ask for the article. But, before you get to that point, be safe and submit a query. *A sample query letter is found on the companion CD-ROM.*

The pertinent press release

One of the most common methods of getting free publicity is to write and send out press releases. Releases must be done correctly, and clearly demonstrate a community benefit to catch the eye of an editor. Your best bet would be to find another angle, rather than just simply talking about your vending business. For example, if your company is the first in your area to vend hot pizzas, pretzels, or other novelty items in a machine, focus your press release around that. If your company is involved in a fund-raising effort for a good cause or sponsors a local sports team that is doing well, write about either of those topics and only mention the company as an afterthought. It will always be best to devote only the last paragraph or two to your company's focus and history. Your press release will have a much better chance to make it into the community pages of your local newspaper if the article does not sound like a free advertising spot.

Always remember to keep press releases short. Most newspapers are tight on space and will typically choose a shorter article over a longer one if editors are faced with deciding between two press releases. If you are unsure of your writing abilities, enlist the aid of a local college student studying journalism and pay him or her a set fee for producing your company's press release. *You will find a sample press release on the companion CD-ROM.*

Once your press release is finished, make sure you do not waste time sending it to the wrong person or department at the newspaper. Study your local paper to find out who covers business or community news and direct the press release to him or her. If your area has more than one newspaper, target them all. You will oftentimes have more luck with a weekly community newspaper, since these tend to have less staff and appreciate receiving news from the residents in their coverage areas.

Smart vending operators can also take advantage of local television coverage in their regions. If your company sponsors a sports team that is doing well, send a press release to the print media and call the television and radio stations in your area. It is exciting to see your company's name on little league or soccer team shirts.

When disaster strikes and there are storm evacuees or other refugees housed in your area, load up a pallet with cases of snacks and canned drinks and head to the church, school, or other facility where they are staying. More than just getting the opportunity to be featured on the 5 p.m. news or in the next day's newspapers, actions like these build you a good rapport with the public, which is the basis of what good public relations is. Moreover, one of the fastest and most brand building methods of marketing and public relations is through word of mouth. If the public notices that you are helping out the community during a difficult situation, they may be more inclined to work with you on future projects. If you are unsure where to go during such situations, call your local chapter of the American Red Cross.

Public relations is also about keeping your current location managers, or clients, content and satisfied. Some ways of doing this include the occasional free or reduced vending snacks for special occasions or meetings. These especially work well around the holidays as a special thank you on your part for the previous year's business. Popping in to see the manager every few weeks is also a good idea, and while you are there, drop off a few snacks you might have removed from the machine because they were about to expire. They will never notice, and the public relations you gain from the act will reap plenty of gratitude.

The occasional phone call will also suffice. Call your location managers on a regular basis to ensure they are satisfied and also to find out if there are any issues you need to be aware of. You might find out that your competition has been by and has offered to undercut your prices or provide a greater commission. Your impromptu phone call might just save you a good location from time to time. Sending out holiday cards is also an inexpensive form of public relations. It will keep your name in front of the location manager and remind him or her of your appreciation.

Keeping Your Paperwork in Order

Your home office will be command central for everything related to the smooth operation of your vending business. It will be the primary resting place for every invoice, route card, tax deposit receipt, canceled check, and any other piece of paper your business generates. You will need to create an organized filing system so you will always have paid and payable invoices close at hand, as well as product catalogs, distributor lists, and other important information. Since you most likely will file your taxes as a sole proprietor or a partner utilizing pass-through taxation for your income, it is extremely important you keep records of all your expenses, such as service vehicle gasoline and repair bills, vendor commissions and charity payments, warehouse rental fees, employee benefit costs (if applicable), and business insurance bills. If you plan on writing off part of your home expenses because it serves as the headquarters of your vending business, you will also need to keep copies of all utility bills and other home expenses for figuring your office percentages at tax time.

If you plan to use a home computer in your business, you can use a specialized business or income tax program for entering these figures throughout the year, which will help you avoid the rush and logjam of information every spring. *See Appendix B for a list of these programs.* All of your meticulous archiving will more than pay for itself come income tax time. If this is the first time you have worked as a sole proprietor, you will be pleasantly surprised to find out your income tax filings will not be drastically different, due to what is known as pass-though taxation. This enables you to claim your business income just as you would the income as an employee on IRS Form 1040, with the exception that you will also need to file Schedule C, which is known as a profit and loss statement.

Self-employment Taxes

One main taxation difference between you as a sole proprietor and an employee is that the employee has income taxes and FICA (social security and Medicare taxes) deducted from his or her pay every two weeks and you do not. Therefore, Uncle Sam requires you to send in your estimated taxes on a quarterly basis. These estimates are usually based on a person's previous year's income, but if you have never worked as a sole proprietor before, you probably have no idea how much money — if any — you will make the first year. If you choose a high number just to be on the safe side, you can probably expect a refund the next year, but the IRS gets to keep your money interest-free in the meantime.

It is imperative you mail in your quarterly tax payments on time. The first quarter tax installment covers the period from January 1 through March 31 and is due by April 15; the second quarter runs from April 1 to May 31 and is due by June 15; the third quarter tax period runs from June 1 to August 31 and payment is due by September 15; and the fourth quarter runs from September 1 to December 31 and is due by January 15 of the following year. If you are late on any quarterly payment or decide to wait until April 15 to pay all your taxes, the IRS will hit you with a 5 percent penalty of the tax owed for each month or part of a month that your return is late, up to five months.

Another important distinction you might now have if you have recently left the ranks of the employed is that you no longer have an employer paying half of your social security and Medicare taxes, which are mutually referred to as self-employment taxes. Thus, your own tax bill will now increase as you take on the entire burden of these taxes. Social security taxes are figured at about 12.4 percent of your company's profits and Medicare (up to a maximum taxable earning of about $106, 800) is taxed at 2.9 percent, with no maximum ceiling. Fortunately, you can deduct half of these taxes from your taxable income when filing your income taxes in April, and you are completely relieved of any self-employment tax liability if you make less than $400 during the year.

Depending on the state in which you live, you might also owe state income tax in April for the profits earned by your vending business the previous year. Some states require estimated quarterly tax payments, like the federal government, so check with your state tax commission on what is expected of you as a sole proprietor.

The Schedule C

Schedule C will enable you to deduct a portion of your home's utility and other bills from your taxable earnings if used for business purpose, such as storing merchandise or using a portion of your home for business. But, navigating these tricky income tax waters have caused many a business owner to flounder and face penalties and/or back taxes. When in doubt about deductions, check with your bookkeeper or tax adviser to make sure you qualify for the deduction you are claiming. The IRS allows you to deduct expenses from the exact part of your home you use for your home-based business, but its rules are strict. For example, if your home office is located in a spare bedroom, that room cannot be used for any other purposes than conducting your business affairs. If it also contains a daybed where someone could potentially spend the night, the IRS would automatically disqualify the deduction. Does that mean the room would have to be sparsely furnished? Not exactly. You could have a television or a stereo in your home office, but it would have to be for the exclusive use of the person conducting business in the name of your company. If your children regularly come in to watch the TV in the afternoon while you work, the room would be disqualified as a deduction. You might ask how the IRS could prove you use the room for other purposes, but the truth is you are the one asking for the deduction. It is not up to the organization to prove anything. It is up to you to prove the room is not used for any other purposes. Granted, you might never have to put out the welcome mat for an IRS agent visiting your home, but if you are ever audited, the agent will ask all the hard questions, and you will be expected to give the right answers.

Should that discourage you from claiming part of your home as a deduction for your home-based vending business? No, but you must be rational about it. For example, Schedule C requires you use the square footage of the part of your home dedicated to your business to figure out its exact percentage of your home in general. Say you have a 1,500-square-foot home and your office is 300 square feet. That is 20 percent of your home's entire living space, so in the eyes of the IRS, you have the legal right to deduct 20 percent of your entire home's utility bills, mortgage payments, maintenance costs, and even cleaning services. The IRS checks these deductions meticulously, so if you are claiming 20 percent of your home's space as an area solely dedicated to business and are deducting 50 percent of the electric bill, you are automatically asking for an audit. If Uncle Sam finds you at fault of trying to deduct more than you deserve, you will not only have to pay back taxes, but penalties, as well.

If you use the garage for your warehouse, you can use its percentage of your home's total space for figuring your deductions, but your vehicles must always remain in the driveway and outside of the garage from then on. The same goes for lawn mowers and other lawn tools and implements. It is wise to use an outside storage shed or patio for storing these types of things once you begin claiming your garage for business purposes. You should probably consider installing a separate phone line used exclusively for the vending business purposes. Otherwise, you will find it difficult — if not impossible — to figure out what percentage of the telephone bill to deduct, and possibly miss important business phone calls if family members tie up the line.

Vehicle Use: Personal or Business?

The same rules apply to deducting expenses for your service vehicle. If you use a step van for your vending business and the vehicle remains parked in your driveway when not being used to service vending routes, you can deduct 100 percent of the mileage, roughly $0.45 per mile. On the other hand, if you use the family van for business, but also use it to ferry the kids to soccer practice, you can only deduct expenses for the actual mileage used in route servicing. Obviously, a dual-purpose vehicle will require much more accurate record keeping, so you might want to opt for a vehicle solely dedicated to the business. Be sure to keep a mileage log in your service vehicle within reach at all times, so you will not forget to notate this valuable deduction. If you drive 5,000 miles a year for business, this deduction alone will cut $2,250 out of your gross sales figure. At a 20 percent tax bracket, that will save you $450 of what you owe.

Appreciate your depreciations

The federal government will allow you to depreciate a service vehicle or other equipment purchased solely for use in your vending business. This means the IRS will allow you to deduct one-seventh of the value of the purchase as a business expense for a total of seven years. If your new vehicle cost $21,000, you can deduct $3,000 annually from your gross income figures. At a 20 percent tax rate, that deduction alone would shave $600 off your taxes each year for seven years. This deduction can be applied to new and used vending machines, warehouse equipment, computers, and printers — in effect, anything that is dedicated solely to your business, but the amount of depreciation time could vary, depending on the item.

Since the IRS is a stickler for proof if you ever get audited, you must make a habit of keeping all receipts for equipment purchased that you plan on depreciating. Set aside a specific file folder for each year's purchases, and make sure you get receipts for any used equipment. Make sure you carry blank receipt forms with you whenever you shop for a used vendor or other equipment in case the seller does not have one. These can be found in most office supply stores or easily designed on a desktop computer. Make the seller sign the receipt, and note his or her address.

Calculating Year-end Inventory

You should make a year-end product inventory a habit, especially because you can write this dollar amount off of your gross income for the tax year. You might find the best time to do this is during the week between Christmas and New Year's Day, when most of your locations are quiet and likely will not need servicing because of the holidays. Make a careful list of each item, the total number of its cases or boxes, and the value for the total number (how much would it cost to replace the cases or boxes). Add up the entire value of your complete inventory, re-check your figures, and file the document with your other important tax papers until April or whenever you usually begin working on your income taxes. If you own any vending computer software, year-end inventory calculating might be included as a feature. If not, you can easily find inventory control and management software through most online software retailers.

Regardless of how much space you claim for your home-based business and how much mileage you write off for your service vehicle, you will need to check and recheck your figures meticulously before mailing off your first income tax papers as a sole proprietor. If you have any doubt as to your accuracy, it is better to call a professional income tax service. The amount you pay the service up front will be small compared to what you could eventually face in fines and back taxes if you make a mistake. The professionals will probably know a few tricks you do not and might end up saving you enough to cover their expert services.

Charles Taylor of VendingRules.com said many new vending operators are tempted not to declare all or part of their income because of the nature of the business. He warns those who call him for vending consultations that they should not try to hoodwink the IRS. This could result in serious repercussions because it is illegal. "The idea of having the all-cash business tempts people to try and get by without paying taxes," he said. "But, right now the government is looking for money wherever it can find it. I report everything so I can sleep well at night."

Automate Your Accounting

Taylor said he discovered throughout the years that many people start a vending business without any formal business training or knowledge of how to keep track of business expenses. "Unfortunately, many people jump into vending without understanding business that well," he said. "Half the time, I end up teaching them basic business principles, such as how to write a cash flow statement, how to tell if they're making a profit, and the difference between hard and soft expenses."

Any sole proprietor worth his or her salt will tell you it is necessary to keep monthly records on your income and expenses to know how you are really doing. Sometimes known as profit and loss statements, these records will help you know just how well (or poorly) your business is doing, as well as provide clues to weak and strong areas. Writing your profit and loss statement can be done manually with a pencil and paper, but you will find it less time-consuming and much neater to use a personal computer and a good software program such as R*KOM's Profit and Loss software (**www.rkom.com/pl.htm**), which even offers a free demo of the software. QuickBooks Pro is a more expensive option (around $200), but the Web site offers a free trial of the software before purchasing (**www.quickbooks.com**), as well as an online version that charges a small monthly fee. If you have time to search the Web, you might find some free downloads that will serve your company. Soft32.com (**www.soft32.com**) offers a good variety of free software, including a spreadsheet for figuring your profits and losses.

No software can help you, though, if you do not gather daily route information and keep good records. This is where you will need the route cards since they record vital information and statistics from each of your vending locations. You can compare sales from consecutive visits, consecutive months, and quarters. With these figures and your computer software program, you will be able to track your sales as a whole from month to month, as well as each location's individual sales. In order to track the latter, you will need to figure out its particular percentage of your company's total gross sales, then subtract the cost of merchandise, sales taxes, location commission (if any), and any other expenses.

For example, say you have 10 locations of snack and cold-drink vendors and you did $150,000 in gross sales for the month of September. Location number three produced $25,000, which is just less than 17 percent of the total. To figure its net profit, the cost of merchandise ($13,755) and 6 percent sales tax ($1,500) must be subtracted. That leaves a net profit of $9,745 from which you must deduct the location's 10 percent commission ($974.50). The final net profit for the location is $8,770.50, a figure that does not reflect the deduction of general business expenses, such as gasoline, office utility bills, freight expenses, and other items. To figure those amounts, you would need to take the month's total general expenses and multiply them by 17 percent to get the location's exact net profit. For convenience sake, say your September general expenses were $680. Seventeen percent of that figure is $115.60 and, when subtracted from $8,770.50, it shows a more accurate net profit of $8,654.90.

Your vending software will do a much quicker job of figuring these percentages than a standard calculator and enable you to compare these figures side-by-side for the week, month, quarter, or year. In this way, you can tell which locations are under- and over-performing and use the merchandise information from the rate cards to learn what product sectors of which locations need tweaking to bring up sales. Keeping all these statistics on paper would require stacks of legal-sized notepads, but with a computer they are all safely stored on your hard drive.

Control Your Costs

Other than increasing sales, one of the easiest ways to increase your bottom line is to more effectively control costs. This is particularly important in the light of today's present economy and rising fuel prices, which are forcing consumers to spend more on gasoline and less on impulse purchases from vending machines. Joe Gilbert, the vice president and general manager of south Florida's vending equipment distributor VE South, said vending operators are especially affected by the squeeze on disposable income. "Vending as a whole is being squeezed very tightly now because they don't have the freedom like retail to change prices indiscriminately," he said. "The small independent vending operator can't increase prices because the locations refuse to let him raise the prices. They tell him, 'You raise the prices and we will get another vending company.' And guess what? There's always somebody out there willing to put it in for a lower price."

Obviously, fuel will be one of your biggest expenses, and its ever-rising cost can do real damage to profits if not properly managed. One of the best ways to protect your profits is to limit the number of unnecessary trips to your locations. This can be done by constantly fine-tuning your route service schedule. Try to resist servicing your larger snack and beverage vendors until they are at least two-thirds empty. It does no good to your bottom line to make a special service call just because one particular candy bar sold out in a particular location.

"The number-one way to save costs is to have a compact, efficient route," Taylor said. "If gas were to drop to a quarter a gallon next week, I would still say the same thing. People spent too much on machines and then spend too much time driving around to the machines. That's what's killing the businesses."

If you have more than one service route, try to service all of the locations that are closer to your office on the same day and lump together the others that might be farther away for servicing a different day. Try to avoid driving more than five or ten minutes between locations, if you can. If there is a possibility that you might have to renegotiate your farthest location because the manager is asking for a bigger cut, consider dumping that one for a closer location. You will not only save gas and service time, but probably also pay less in commissions. You might find 20 smaller, nearby locations to be more profitable than 15 larger ones requiring more frequent servicing and more trips to the gas pump.

Bruce Adams of Rainbow Vending Inc. of Denver has fine-tuned his vending business down to a compact route of approximately 20 locations, about 80 percent of which he services twice a week. Because his company's fuel bills have steadily increased over the years, he has gotten smarter about his vending machines. "Now we try and go and buy the biggest equipment we can find," he said.

Charles Taylor said he frequently counsels vendors over the phone whose primary problem is the distance and time they are dedicating to their locations. "I had two people call me and tell me they were having trouble making ends meet," he said. "The problem was they were spending all day to do just three or four locations. Those four locations should only take you two hours at most. Obviously, you want all the machines as close together as possible. I turn things away now all the time because they're too far away from my route."

If you have the storage space, you can also cut some costs by purchasing products in larger quantities to get a deeper price cut. Be wary, though, of stockpiling too many items that could potentially go out of date and end up costing you more money in the long run. Before buying in bulk, carefully study the route cards of your locations to see if you can move that much merchandise on time. Taylor said he has never found buying in bulk to be a successful strategy. Instead, he prefers to concentrate more on equipment costs and route management.

Outfitting Your Home Office

Although it is entirely possible to run your vending business the old-fashioned way with pen and paper, you will find it much easier and less time-consuming to incorporate the latest technology in the day-to-day operations of your new business. The most crucial elements to your home office should be a desktop computer and a quality printer.

Although you do not need the most powerful personal computer on the planet, you will be better off buying one that has enough memory and speed to run specialized vending software and other programs needed for business operations. Your printer is also one area you will not want to skimp on. Your best bet is to skip the prepackaged combinations of printer and computer because they tend to bundle a less-expensive printer with the deal. Instead, buy the pieces separately so you can purchase a device that not only prints, but also scans, photocopies, and sends and receives faxes. This will save you from having to buy a separate fax machine, since some companies want orders and other communications faxed instead of e-mailed.

Many people nowadays are opting for a powerful laptop rather than a desktop computer, since it can play double duty as a home PC and a traveling workstation. If you buy a smaller laptop, you might wish to also buy a larger keyboard that plugs into one of the Universal Serial Bus (USB) terminals of your laptop, since you might tire of typing on the laptop's more compact keyboard. You might also want to buy a separate USB mouse, since laptops usually incorporate a tiny button or touch pad to control the movement of the curser.

There are many online sources for buying computers and peripherals. One of the most aggressive of these companies is TigerDirect (**www.tigerdirect.com**), which continuously offers closeout prices on a variety of computers, laptops, and other devices. Be wary of signing up for newsletters from these companies, however, as they tend to constantly bombard your inbox with offers. You will also find the BizRate Web site to be invaluable for comparing prices on computers and a variety of other office equipment (**www.bizrate.com**). *You will find a brief list of these in Appendix B under "Computers and Peripherals."*

If you do not already have a desk, you can find one at many of the office supply stores for around $100. Most of these come with large slide-out keyboard shelves, as well as with smaller shelves for books, computer speakers, and other items. Remember that most new desks require assembly. If you do not want to commit the time to this project, you can also look for an already-assembled used desk at a garage sale or on Craigslist.

An answering machine is another essential item you will want for your home office, especially since you will frequently be away from the telephone when servicing your vending locations. The last thing you will want is to miss an important call from a potential location manager. A small filing cabinet will also prove useful for archiving your paid invoices and accounts payable, vendor location contracts, charity organization and location commission agreements, and other important papers.

Do not forget the basics, such as a surge protector, printer and fax paper, stationary and envelopes (preferably with your company's own letterhead), a stapler, and a variety of writing instruments. You can refer to the following checklist for office supplies essential to the smooth operation of your vending business.

Essential Office Supplies Checklist

- Computer, monitor, keyboard, and mouse
- Combination printer, scanner, copier, and fax
- Surge protector
- Optional vending business software programs
- Printer and fax paper (if applicable)
- Computer desk and chair
- Adding machine with tape feature
- Small file cabinet or file boxes
- Answering machine
- High-intensity reading lamp
- Pre-printed stationary and envelopes with your letterhead
- Business cards
- Coin and bill counters (if applicable)
- Coin and currency wrappers
- Stapler
- Rolodex or other type of business card holder
- Pens, pencils, and other writing instruments

Chapter Takeaways

Unfortunately, the work is not over yet. There are still a few more items that need to be handled before you can call it day. These are considered off-road requirements because these tasks are handled back at the office. Although these items might not seem as glamorous as their on-road counterparts, they are nonetheless extremely important to the success of your business operations. Before kicking back in the recliner and slipping into your "comfies," be sure you have handled these off-road requirements.

- Consider your coin-counting options carefully

- Continue to develop, revamp, and implement a strategic marketing plan for your business

- Keep important paperwork easily accessible and neatly organized

- Keep adequate records of your income, expenses, and inventory to stay on course toward a profitable financial future

- Equip your office with the most efficient and cost-effective equipment, which does not have to be the best, most expensive technology

CHAPTER 12

Exploring Other Options

Say you are extremely interested in the vending industry, but are not sure if you are ready to take the entrepreneurial plunge on your own. Fortunately, there are other choices for you to experience the industry without having to go out on a limb.

Getting Your Feet Wet

If you are semi-retired or looking for a career change, you might want to consider taking a job as a vending route driver. Most of the country's larger vending companies hire employees to service their machines. This position would give you the opportunity to see if you like the kind of work involved. Although you would not be doing any of the merchandise ordering or paying the bills, you would be experiencing the most labor-intensive part of the business. You would also learn many of the skills necessary in running your own vending business, such as how to stock a service vehicle, properly load snack and drink vendors, remove proceeds and refill coin magazines, do simple maintenance, and clean the machines. You might even get some experience dealing with location managers, which could prove invaluable in the future for launching your own vending firm.

You could also use your time as a route driver to check out some potential locations, noting which appear underserved or which ones might be good for a niche product. If you want to learn the managerial skills necessary for running your own business, you could potentially work your way up the vending ladder to the head office. There, you would learn all about finding and maintaining locations, ordering merchandise and inventory control, and accounts payable and receivable. Once you rise to the top, you might find that is where you want to be; if not, you will have learned all the skills necessary to be the sole proprietor of your own vending operation. To find vending route driver positions in your area, check the classified advertisements of the industry publication and Web sites, such as **www.vendingconnection.com**.

One of the best ways to find out how you would succeed as an independent vending operator is to try your hand as a locator. Since this job requires you to meet constantly with the public, a good appearance is important. A sales background is also beneficial, but not absolutely necessary. Most locators do come from a sales background and are used to knocking on enough doors to get a positive response. However, some successful vending operators, such as Chris Robertson of Toronto Vending Services, learned locating the hard way: by having doors slammed in his face.

"I had so many people telling me, 'No, we're sorry, but we already have machines,' or, 'We are not interested,'" he said. "I had so many doors closed in my face…it was very discouraging. Then I would get a location, and that would give me the confidence to go out and get another." Through his persistence, Robertson built his business up from one vendor and one location nine years ago to 35 locations today. He thinks locating is the biggest challenge for any vending operator starting out. Today, he shares his success via his Web site (**www.myvendingsecret.com**) and an e-book, *Vending Business Tactics*.

One of the easiest ways to get experience as a locator is to contact one of the large locating companies, most of which advertise in the classified sections of vending trade organization Web sites. These firms usually pay a set fee for a specific number of locations obtained and might be willing to give a novice a try. Be forewarned: They probably will not pay anything if you come back empty handed. If you become successful at spotting out locations for others, you will have overcome the primary obstacle for most vending entrepreneurs. If you choose to pursue a vending career as an operator afterward, your own success would be almost guaranteed.

Providing the Industry Infrastructure

If you have a background in sales, you will most likely have no problem dealing with location managers and securing locations for vendors. You might also find, as Eric Normand of UsedVending.com did, that there is a huge market and need for vending equipment infrastructure to support the industry. Instead of meeting those needs, the biz-op and blue-sky promoters are simply dumping a glut of overpriced vendors on the market. These machines frequently end up collecting dust in a garage or warehouse, but since most are hardly even used, they can still bring a handsome price on the used equipment market.

Although Normand eventually sold his vending operation to avoid a potential conflict and to devote himself more fully to his equipment business, many operators successfully run vending routes and buy and sell equipment at the same time. Bruce Adams of Rainbow Vending has built up an all-around business by incorporating vending, new and used equipment sales, vendor repair, and the sale of locations. Joe Gilbert of VE South in Fort Lauderdale, Florida, has spent his entire career in the equipment side of the vending industry. Working his way up from parts manager of a Connecticut jukebox distributor, Gilbert became the regional sales director for the largest vending equipment manufacturers and distributors in the nation.

Star Foods, the United States Department of Agriculture compliance program, enables large schools to serve more complete meals in less time through vending machines that sell the same quality meals as the cafeteria. The vendors incorporate card-reader technology and pin-pads, which enable students to buy without cash and correctly identify all those qualified for the free or reduced lunch programs. They are also intelligent, using telemetry to communicate with the food service office when they are low or out of certain foods.

"The schools make the lunches that have to adhere to the USDA regulations," he said. "The Star Food gives the school districts an opportunity to feed more kids by placing the machines through-out various areas of the campus. There is a school in Burke County, Georgia that is feeding up to 300 more students per day out of a 1,200 student school population. The student reaches in and grabs a package that has a complete meal in less than 20 seconds."

Take a repair course

If you are somewhat mechanically inclined, another way to get in through the back door of the vending industry is through repair work. Many vending operators do not have time to repair their machines once their routes have grown, so they must contract outside repairmen for anything other than minor problems fixable by a route driver. Once you earn a reputation for providing quality work at good prices, you might be one of the most popular men or women in town.

To find a training course in your area, check **www.vendingconnection.com**, industry trade publications, and your local community college to see if it offers a vending repair training course. You should also check to see if there are already any vending repair companies nearby. Some of these, such as Bob's Vending Repair Service in Bedford, Texas, offer training courses on the side. According to his company's Web site (**www. bvrsales.com**), owner Bob Weeks offers courses on Saturdays in the Dallas-Fort Worth area that cover everything from troubleshooting the basics to advanced repairs. Weeks also offers one-on-one classes and teaches all facets of the industry to those just starting out as vending operators, including which equipment would be best for their particular situations. If your local vending repair company does not offer courses, it might be willing to hire you and train you for the job, providing you another avenue of entrance into the profession.

If none of the above applies to where you live, you can still become a certified vending technician through an at-home technician training program offered by the National Automated Merchandising Association (NAMA). NAMA's dual-focus program enables anyone to become a certified vending technician or a technician by studying the respective fundamentals manual, along with the electrical or electronics manual and passing the exams.

If you happen to be mechanically inclined, you could learn to repair machines on your own. Chris Robertson of Toronto Vending Services learned how to repair vendors by having a great relationship with his local vending equipment distributor. "I would call him, and he would tell me what to do over the phone," he said. "Or, I would go over there and he would show me what to do and get me the part. Then I would go back to fix it. We were working together towards a common goal. I was buying my machines from him, and I was building my business."

Put on a trade show

If you work well with the public, you could think about going to work for NAMA or one of the other vending trade organizations or event planners that put together the various vending industry trade shows and conferences throughout the year. This behind-the-scenes work would introduce you to the biggest names in the industry in areas from equipment manufacturers and distributors to locating companies, repair companies, and supply companies. You would also be one of the first to glimpse some of the hottest new vending ideas and trends on the market. A job planning such events would provide you a vending education unlike any other and give you an information edge over anyone else starting out in the industry.

Chapter Takeaways

Starting your own vending company can be a risky business. Do not worry if you are not quite ready to take the full plunge. Being a successful entrepreneur will take a lot of hard work, diligence, and stamina. If you are not sure at this point, consider several of the options that were discussed in this chapter, and remember these few tips:

- Consider taking a job as a vending route driver

- If you want to know for sure if you will be good as a vending entrepreneur, try being a locator

- For the mechanically inclined, get in through the back door of the vending industry by taking a vending repair training course

- If you are more public relations oriented, consider putting on a trade show for one of the vending trade organizations

CHAPTER 13

The Future of Vending

The future of the $22 billion vending machine industry is fraught with challenges and full of the promise of innovation. To succeed in the future, both new vending operators and those who have been in the industry for years will have to adapt and be more creative than in the past, due to a more challenging economic scenario. Operators increasingly find themselves caught in the vise of rising fuel prices and the inability to effectively raise snack and drink prices, due to fierce resistance from both location managers and consumers with less disposable income. According to *Automatic Merchandiser* magazine's "2008 State of the Vending Industry" report, the vending and food service industries have experienced four poor years in a row, with most operators now shifting into survival mode.

Survey Finds Operators in Balancing Act

For its report, *Automatic Merchandiser* surveyed a cross section of full-line vending operators located throughout the United States and analyzed data from product and equipment suppliers and governmental entities. The report found the majority of operators have begun to take a variety of measures, both positive and negative, to shore up the bottom line. Almost 60 percent of operators surveyed have reduced their deliveries or cut back their service frequency to save on unnecessary fuel costs, while the same amount said they were tweaking the merchandise mix in machines to have sufficient stock of the more popular items. Some vending operators are removing underperforming equipment from locations, while others are adding vendors to locations to be able to reduce the frequency of service. Small to mid-size companies have continued a trend of buying out the competition to increase volume and sales and alleviate competitive pressure.

Roughly 25 percent of the operators said they were adding services to increase profits, with about 35 percent adding office coffee service to their vending mix. About 30 percent have begun shipping or delivering products to non-vending customers in what is frequently called wholesale delivery. These are generally smaller retail and dining establishments that do not sell enough of the products to warrant the services of a regular distributor, but still want the convenience of having them delivered to their place of business.

The rising cost of doing business and maintaining the status quo are also inhibiting businesses from investing in new technologies necessary to compete against their primary competitors: convenience stores. These include cashless machines, which accept both debit and credit cards for payment, and the use of telemetry. Although a few of the largest operators have been incorporating both into their businesses, the hefty initial investment takes a substantial amount of time to recoup, which is inhibiting smaller and mid-size companies from using them.

Vending's largest segment, cold drinks, is what hindered profitability for many full-line operators in 2007, according to the report. Retail machine price increases were frequently insufficient to cover the rise in the wholesale price of bottled beverages. This is one reason many operators have tried to add more canned drinks, which allow greater room for price increases, to their beverage mix. Environmentally aware consumers are also opting for more canned beverages for the first time since plastic bottles were introduced in the 1990s. This consumer segment considers plastic bottles environmentally unfriendly, while aluminum cans are highly recyclable.

Cold drink operators are also finding it difficult to keep up with other consumer beverage trends, such as energy or sports drinks. While a convenience store can stock an almost unlimited variety of beverages, most drink vending machines are limited to just a few selections. This forces operators to make difficult marketing choices or avoid the trends altogether, unless they are able to provide multiple vendors for their locations.

In the full-service line, hot beverage machine sales are declining in tandem with the downsizing of factories and other large workplaces. Many of these vendors are being gradually replaced with office coffee service, one of the industry's fastest-growing segments, although specialty coffee machines are also seeing success in some locations. Frozen prepared foods grew slightly in 2007, while freshly prepared food vendor sales declined. The only segment steadily growing is that of integrated food systems, in which vendors keep the foods or ingredients frozen until the sale and then have a separate preparation apparatus that prepares them for immediate consumption. These systems, which have grown steadily in sales for seven years, include such items as pizza and freshly prepared ice cream.

According to the report, much of the vending industry is stagnating because operators have so far failed to adapt to a changing marketplace and still rely on a business model that depends on large industrial work sites. With the downsizing of factories and many jobs being sent abroad, the industry's primary customer base has been steadily shrinking. The problem is that the largest operators continue to focus on such locations, with manufacturing vending locations actually growing from 28.4 percent in 2004 to 36.2 percent of total sales in 2007. The report recommended favoring the potential of small to mid-size companies, which are more willing to service smaller accounts or provide to vending locations in sectors other than manufacturing.

Niche Marketing: Find the Next Wave

Vending entrepreneurs will continue to find future success in meeting the specific needs of a particular segment of the population. The California company Yo-Naturals (**www.yonaturals. com**) is another unique vending operator. Yo-Naturals is riding the healthy snack and beverage wave started by a federal mandate requiring vending machines in schools to offer more healthy alternatives. Instead of just a certain percentage of healthy snacks, however, the San Diego company is taking the healthy snack movement even further by placing vendors that exclusively offer a variety of natural and organic snacks and drinks. The products feature the biggest names in the natural and organic food movement, such as Horizon™ organic milk products, Stacy's and Terra snack foods, FIJI® spring water, Pirate's Booty, and many others. The company offers both snack and drink machines, as well as a combination machine for smaller locations. All of the vendors, referred to as kiosks by the company, are state-of-the-art and utilize cashless payment systems that accept both debit and credit cards, and are wired for remote monitoring. Yo-Naturals has found a ready market in schools, health clubs, gymnasiums, and other locations and is looking for operators interested in the company's kiosks to expand in areas outside its present service area.

Two young men from New Jersey also found out things were not particularly "kosher" in the vending world, and so launched their New York firm, Kosher Vending Industries. Doron Fetman and Alan Cohnen had already been distributing Glatt Kosher foods for several years, but decided that much of the traveling Jewish population was being underserved. Today, just two years after placing their first "Hot Nosh" and "Kosher Café" vendors, the company services more than 100 machines in locations ranging from sports arenas and shopping centers to John F. Kennedy Airport. Kosher Vending (**www.koshervendingindustries.com**) offers two kinds of vendors, one dedicated exclusively to vending three types of kosher hot dogs, and the other offering everything from deep-dish cheese pizza to potato knishes and veggie cutlets. Future food choices might also soon include quiches, pocket sandwiches, baked ziti, blintzes, and breakfast burritos. The vendors keep the products frozen until the point of sale, and then microwave them for 90 seconds. The average vend is $3 and the machines accept debit and credit cards for payment. Company staff can also remotely monitor the vendors through telemetry.

Kosher Vending now has vendors placed as far away as Boston's Fenway Park and is currently in talks with companies in both Los Angeles and Las Vegas. The company and its backers see a growing demand for kosher products in many areas that are not currently being served. According to the Kosher Vending Web site, kosher products are a $165 billion industry and the "kosher market has been growing at an annual rate of 15 percent for the past several years." The company sees itself fulfilling the vending needs of those who otherwise would have to make do with a much less-satisfying food option.

Technology and target marketing

As both the Yo-Naturals and Kosher Vending companies have demonstrated, both an investment in technology and a truly focused and defined market hold the keys to potential success in the vending industry. Although the latter can eventually be determined by sufficiently studying the area market, the former has been out of the financial reach of all but the largest of vending companies for years. Cashless vending machines like those used by the aforementioned companies are cost prohibitive for most new vending operators, and even industry veterans decry the lengthy time it would take to recoup their initial equipment investment. Some of the industry's hottest new ideas, such as the French fry and pizza machines, are extremely expensive and require frequent servicing.

A 2004 article published in *Nation's Restaurant News* addressed the issue of technology in the vending industry by interviewing many of the vending operators attending NAMA's semi-annual vending that year. Both operators and distributors spoke out in the article, saying that technology was running way ahead of an industry in which operators had yet to see a potential payoff for such expensive equipment investments. As a result, even six years later, consumers in most of the small or mid-sized vending locations are still not seeing a lot of these types of machines. Rather than relying on such innovative technology, smaller vending operators in the future will have to concentrate on more productive locations, larger vendor capacity, and less frequent servicing to improve their profit margins.

Chapter Takeaways

With any entrepreneurial endeavor, it is a necessity to find creative ways to make your business stand out above the competition. You might find the perfect niche, but ultimately that niche will require your time, energy, and undivided attention. Not just in the world of vending, but in the world of business, it is imperative to not let your business stagnate. Think ahead and look for new and improved ways to make your company unique.

- Learn to keep your business afloat during the drought times

- Research the industry trends and try to tailor your vending products to match those trends

- The two primary keys to success in the vending industry are to invest in technology and focus on a specific market

- Consider going to a cashless payment vendor that accepts both debit and credit cards

- To successfully ride the next wave of vending, consider expanding in areas outside your present service area

CHAPTER 14

Putting the Pieces Together

Now that you have gotten this far, you have filled up your head with a lot of information that needs to be sorted out. One of the most important lessons you need to remember when contemplating operating a vending business is to avoid getting caught up in the heady rush of the biz-op, blue-sky promoters. Unfortunately, being hoodwinked is one of the most common ways people start off in the vending industry. The biz-op promoters truly do paint a beautiful blue-sky panorama of the industry with a pot of cash at the end of every vending rainbow. What they will not tell you is that the earnings figures they quote are from established operators who have been in the industry for years and placed their vendors in the best locations in the country. If they were to show the true sales figures for people just starting out, they would hook far fewer people into investing their life savings in just a handful of vendors. In case you need a reminder, go back and read through the case studies of UsedVending.com and VendingRules.com to refresh your memory. A biz-op sales pitch is designed to do sell you something that is "too good to be true."

In spite of the black eye those promoters have occasionally given to the industry, vending continues to be a marvelous way in which to make a living or to supplement your present income while still maintaining your independence. It does, however, require a lot more selling than most people are led to believe. Although the machines are the ones marketing and selling the products, you must sell your business (and these machines) to the locations — without which there is no business.

Eric Normand of UsedVending.com said blue-sky promoters propagate one of the industry's greatest fallacies among would-be vending operators: No customer service is required. "If they think that 'All I have to do is go and fill the machines,' they are wrong," he said. The bright side is that many locations are dissatisfied with what they see as impersonal and inefficient service on the part of their current vendors, which is the perfect opportunity for a new operator to get his or her foot in the door. All it takes is willingness to try and keeping a smile on your face, even when potential clients say no. If you keep trying long enough, somebody will eventually say yes.

Business Mentality Required

Remember that on top of everything you do, your new business needs to make a profit. Breaking even in a new business usually takes between two and three years, but that might not apply to a vending operator. Unlike a retail business, a vending operator is not bound by the overhead of renting an expensive commercial property: The highest expenses will be the vendors, the actual products, and the gasoline to service the route. What you have to do is take a hard look at your vendor's cost, your other expenses, and the realistic projected revenue. From there, you need to decide if the profit is a sufficient enough motivator for you to make that initial investment. The desire to make a profit sooner rather than later is the reason many first-time operators refuse to go into debt with overpriced new machines and decide to purchase used ones.

Just as in any business, it is always wiser to grow slowly and steadily. Instead of jumping into vending with both feet, stick your little toe in with a couple of snack vendors or a few bulk machines and see how you progress in the industry. Service and stock your machines well, count your proceeds, and decide if it is worth your time investment. Charles Taylor said one of the most common mistakes new operators make is to completely discount the hours spent servicing the machines. "Your soft costs are your time, and most vendors don't take that into account," he said. "Vendors may spend five or six hours and bring home $100 or less."

Although $20 an hour might sound good to some people, many of those being asked by blue-sky promoters to invest thousands of dollars are being led to believe the pay is much better. One woman whom Taylor counseled over the phone had invested most of her savings in expensive vendors after her husband died. She had never worked outside of the home and was hoping to use the vendors to provide a source of income, but knew nothing about locating them and panicked. Taylor bought a few of them from her to help her out. "You've got to first get your life together before you get your business together," he said. "She had a legal degree. For crying out loud, you can make a lot more money as a paralegal or something."

Taylor emphasized that vending operators need to have goals and even an exit strategy if the need arises. You need to know where you want to go with your business, and that is one reason a well-orchestrated business plan and mission statement are so important. By putting your present financial situation down on paper and mapping out the first few years of your vending business, you will know if you have the financial wherewithal to survive on your own or if you will need outside backing or a partner. If your plan is to buy an existing vending operation, you will need to decide how you want to run your business and set up your legal documentation accordingly. To do this, check with your local and state governments before starting your business. This includes obtaining the necessary business licenses, permits and filling out the necessary sales tax paperwork, if applicable. Nothing would be more frustrating than starting and succeeding in your new business, only to find out you did not follow the correct legal procedures.

Location, Location, Location

The importance of good locations in the vending industry cannot be emphasized enough. One of the biggest problems people discover after falling for a biz-op promoter's sales pitch is that the locations, which they purchased from the biz-op promoter, are either underperforming at best, or are nonexistent in the worst-case scenario. Promoters hire independent contractors to find locations quickly and cheaply and might not have a vested interest in your business. Their interest is to locate your machines with the least amount of time and effort since they are working on a set fee per location. If they really took the time to closely study each location, they might discover, as some brand-new operators do afterward, that the factory had been scheduled to close for a year or the company is slated for massive layoffs. As Eric Normand of UsedVending.com said, "[The effort a locator puts into finding good locations for your vending machines is] usually either not done at all or done so poorly that operators end up thinking, 'What can I do now?'"

Bill Way, a successful operator-turned-vending-machine-distributor and author of *Vending Success Secrets: How Anyone Can Grow Rich In America's Best Cash Business*, says in his book that "there are so few [locating companies] that are worthy of your time and money" that you should consider all vending locators "absolutely worthless." Way said he knows a couple of professional locating companies that are "okay," but refused to list them in his book for fear that something about them would change after publication.

You, on the other hand, have a vested interest in your company and will reap the benefits from a location long after it is secured. That is all the more reason you should be the one pounding the pavement in search of good locations. It will be a different story once your route has grown and prospered so much that locating on your own would take you away from servicing your vendors for too long. By that time, though, you will know what makes a good location and can help guide your locator toward exactly the kind of places that meet the needs of your business. When scouring your own area for potential locations, it is best to create and use a checklist to ensure that they have sufficient employee and/ or customer traffic to warrant your services, particularly if you are placing full-size vendors.

Your Vendors and Style of Vending

Charles Taylor said he found out the hard way that keeping all of his vendors placed was a lot more difficult than buying them in the first place. He and his partner, his wife Laurie, quickly learned their "locations were their assets and not their machines."

In his book, *The Vending Jackpot*, successful North Carolina bulk operator-turned-author Ronnie Talent walks people through the process of buying used vendors for half the price or less from operators who fell for blue-sky scams and never got off the ground. He advises negotiators to secure their vending locations before making their final offer for the machines. All successful vending business owners will tell you that vendors will do you no good sitting in your garage or warehouse. Taylor said the type of machine is not important compared with the type of location.

Before you choose your style of vendors, you must first choose your style of vending. If you are short on investment cash, the easiest way to get your foot in the vending door is with honor box systems. You will also find that it is relatively easy to secure locations for these since most smaller offices and companies are overlooked by the larger vending operations that need a bigger customer base to support the cost of large snack and soda vendors. You will have some shrinkage or theft, but the high profit margins and low overhead of the boxes will still enable you to make a good profit. Due to their relatively small size, honor boxes must be serviced at least every couple of weeks; therefore, they do not work for those short on time to devote to the business.

Bulk vendors require the least amount of effort for the money, since they must only be serviced every month or two. A substantial amount of machines is usually required to see a lot of profit because the average amount of money earned per vendor is approximately $15 to $35 per month, depending on the location. Bulk vendors cost considerably less than snack and cold drink vendors, enabling most entrepreneurs to start out with several. Once again, the key here is to secure the locations before you invest in a lot of bulk vendors, otherwise the only thing they might be gathering is dust in your garage. The snack food and cold drink sectors offer the highest amount of profit per machine, but cost a lot more money and require substantially more time for servicing. Operators must have enough time to devote to servicing their machines regularly, so they are not necessarily the best vending sector for those who are still working a full-time job. Full-line vending, which adds sandwiches, salads, ice cream, and pizza to the mix is the most complicated sector, requiring much more labor-intensive work due to the handling of perishable foods. As a result, this sector is recommended only for those who already have a lot of vending experience under their belts. Finally, you can simply launch out into vending with a product that no one else has tried to vend before. When tackling a new sector in the industry, there are no guarantees for success and you might find it harder to get off the ground. However, all it takes is a little ingenuity and market analysis to solve a common problem or need.

Once you decide on your own personal style of vending, you must determine if you will use charity sponsorships, offer locations commissions, or use location contracts. Each of these is a personal decision and must be made after a careful study of your local area, the present competition, and the types of locations that you are seeking. Remember that if you decide to use location contracts, keep them simple to avoid scaring off potential locations with technical and legal jargon.

Transporting and Managing Your Goods

A dependable service vehicle is essential to placing and servicing your vendors at their respective locations. If you are starting off with a small honor box or bulk-vending business, you can probably get by with the family minivan for a while, but once you grow into other vending sectors or if you start out as a full-line vendor, a larger and sturdier vehicle is a necessity. A full-size panel van or step van are the two most common vending vehicles and most will fit your needs when you are just starting out. While the former is more economical on fuel, the latter makes stocking and servicing vendors a breeze due to the ample headroom and interior aisle.

Once you get your vending company up and running, you must learn how to properly track your inventory and sales to maintain fresh stock in your vendors. It only takes a few stale snacks to give your machine and your company a bad reputation and potentially ruin an otherwise profitable location. Route cards should become your best tools to carefully analyze what products sell the most, determine which ones do not deserve an entire row in a vendor, and to tell how often you need to reorder stock. There are even computer software programs that can help you design planograms, or schematics of your vendors pinpointing exactly which products go where for more efficient vendor servicing. Par sheets, which show the level of merchandise needed on-hand to trigger a re-order for each vending item, are commonly used for more efficient warehousing of stock.

You must also be careful to protect your perishable products, such as chocolates and baked goods, from the ravages of hot summer temperatures. If you use your garage for product storage, the easiest way is to buy a good used refrigerator to store them in. You should also keep a large ice chest, preferably one that has wheels, in your service for storing and transporting your perishables from the vehicle to your vendors. To be a success in vending, you must also be successful in customer service through the implementation of a dependable refund policy at each of your locations. Make sure it is clear with each of your location managers who the refund contact person is and that he or she is fully aware of those duties.

Stepping out of your service vehicle at the end of your route will probably mean the beginning of many other chores rather than the end of a day's work. In addition to sorting and counting your proceeds of the day and making a bank deposit, you will also need to prepare your vehicle for the following day's route. Once that is done, you might need to unpack new merchandise deliveries, organize your warehouse, or prepare new merchandise orders. Office chores might also await, such as checking your e-mail for potential new locations or service issues, paying invoices, and arranging for any needed vendor repairs. This will also be the time you create and implement any marketing and public relations strategies, both of which should be aimed at securing new, profitable locations and keeping your present ones content.

To Grow or Not to Grow

Once your vending business has grown to the point that you are unable to do any more on your own, you must decide if you if you are content with your lifestyle and earnings as a sole proprietor. Many solo operators thrive on the challenge of managing an entire business without any outside help and would have trouble delegating responsibilities or authority to an employee or business partner. If that sounds like you, you are probably best keeping the business the way it is, with simply fine-tuning your locations now and then.

If you are one of those who thrive on the next big challenge, perhaps you have reached the point of hiring either part- or full-time help. In addition to interviewing applicants and making hiring decisions, bringing employees into the fold will bring you all the new challenges and decisions you could possibly want. You will have to learn how to plan employee schedules and do payroll taxes, decide whether or not to offer company benefits, and prepare wage and tax statements at the end of the year. If all of this seems like too much, you might want to first consider hiring part-time help to either do stocking or to accompany you on your route to help you get your vendors serviced in a shorter length of time. In that way, you can gradually learn the ropes of being an employer and decide if you want to grow your business in that way in the future.

Taking on a partner is another option that comes with its own set of particular challenges. Although a partner might come accompanied by a significant cash investment, you will also have to begin dividing the profits accordingly. Depending on the type of partner (general or silent) you choose, he or she may have the right to make and influence business decisions, so you will be giving up your privileged role as commander and chief. There is always the inherent risk that a partner could do damage to the business and the reputation you have nurtured since the beginning, so you should think hard and long before making such a pivotal decision. Consider doing both background and credit checks on any potential candidates.

Finally, you should make use of all of the available options for outside business advice to help you grow your business properly. The U.S. Small Business Administration is a great source for free advice and seminars, and you will find a lot of help from experienced fellow operators. If none in your own area are willing to talk to you, there are a host of online vendors who have written books on their experiences and even offer telephone consultations. *Be sure and check the listings in Appendix B.* Vending industry organizations and their respective trade publications provide a wealth of information and insight into the successful operation and growth of a vending business.

A Choice of Vending Careers

The vending industry has been around for decades, and as a result provides many different avenues of employment, most of which are perfect for introducing the field to those unsure of the industry or their desire to be a sole proprietor. These options include employment as a vending route driver, finding vending locations for operators, working for a manufacturer or distributor, learning to repair vending machines, and working for vending trade show organizers. Many of these career options provide a back-door entrance into the vending field and much of the necessary knowledge needed to be successful as a vending operator. Whether you plan on starting your vending business as a hobby and part-time source of income, or plan on devoting yourself completely to your new endeavor, you should know that many vending operators have successfully implemented vending as just a part of their entrepreneurial activities. Other successful operators have easily combined vending with their other businesses.

One of the most common ways to branch out among operators is through the buying and selling of used vending machines. In the course of their own search for used vending equipment, these entrepreneurs have realized the wealth of good-quality used vendors that are available on the market. Many of these are still in their boxes because their owners never learned how to locate on their own and lost their original locations supplied by the biz-op promoters. The marketing of these vendors has become a profitable new revenue stream for many operators. Some, like Eric Normand of UsedVending.com who also now sells new vendors, have switched completely to this sector of the industry. Other operators, such as Bruce Adams of Rainbow Vending of Denver, have learned to carve different revenue streams out of various vending business sectors to augment the income derived from the vendors themselves. "We do vending, office coffee service, refrigeration, and machine repair," he said. "We sell new and used equipment, and then the last spoke of the wheel is the buying and selling of locations."

Once you successfully launch your own vending business, the confidence and skills you learn along the way might be the impetus you need to ignite your entrepreneurial spark and branch out into other profitable ventures. Charles Taylor, of **www.vendingrules.com**, called these the "basic business concepts" that he could use to succeed in any other type of service business. "I could take the word 'vending' out of this entire discussion and put any other business in there," he said. "The same rules would apply. I could take a lawn service business from zero to $50,000 a year using the same principles."

Once you have written your mission statement and business plan, contacted several potential locations in your area to discover the local vending needs, priced the number and types of vendors you want to install, and gotten your finances in order, it is time to put action behind your entrepreneurial vision and start vending.

CONCLUSION

With the rising cost of gasoline and vending products, many operators are beginning to feel the squeeze of financial pressure and are looking for ways in which to improve their bottom lines. Some are abandoning the old full-line standards, such as hot beverage vendors, due to declining sales, opting instead to provide the less-expensive and labor-intensive office coffee service. Most are finding ways to reduce service frequency, either by adding larger capacity vendors or dropping out of underperforming locations. Others are looking for more profitable segments, such as canned drinks, which are slowly making a comeback and growing in popularity among the environmentally conscious public. Vending entrepreneurs and more entrenched operators are also looking to find more niche markets, such as items marketed toward specific interests groups, genders, healthy snacks, and kosher foods to differentiate their companies from the majority of vending operations. Innovative vendors and cutting-edge technology are there for those operators that are able to invest, but many smaller companies will have to be content without trendy vendors, cashless payment options, or remote monitoring systems unless they have substantial financial backing.

The vending business and the entrepreneurial lifestyle are not for everyone. You might find you prefer the stability of regular office hours and punching a clock to the unpredictability and long hours of managing every aspect of a business yourself. But, you might also find that being untied from the constraints of a nine-to-five job (an office cubicle, a more structured work day, or punching the time clock) and exploring a new scenic route each day is freshly invigorating. The only way for you to find out is to emerge entirely from your comfort zone and take the first necessary step. The second step is always easier and leads to a new realm of self-exploration that you would never have experienced otherwise. Regardless of whether you become a successful vending entrepreneur or not, you will have launched yourself on a road to self-discovery filled with new surprises around every turn.

APPENDIX A

Sample Business Plan

Snack Break Vending, general partnership
BUSINESS PLAN
September 2010
Confidential

Development Team
Rolando and Gloria Garcia
2266 Venture Avenue
San Antonio, Texas
Telephone (777) 777-7777
Web site: www.snackbreakvending.com

Mission Statement

Snack Break Vending is a new vending services company founded to serve the smaller companies and businesses in southern Bexar County (San Antonio) with honor boxes and soda, snack, and coffee vending machines. Vending locations with fewer than 20 employees and no outside traffic will receive an honor box snack system and drink system, if needed. Larger companies or those with outside customer traffic will be provided with modern table-top or free-standing vendors stocked with fresh, guaranteed products. Snack Break Vending will build a niche market among the locations frequently overlooked by larger vending operations because of their limited size.

Executive Summary

Snack Break Vending is a start-up vending operation to be based in southern Bexar County (San Antonio), Texas, and will operate primarily along the I-410 corridor, servicing small, white-collar businesses and companies catering to tourists and the traveling public. Owned by Rolando and Gloria Garcia, the company will operate as a partnership with both partners filing jointly via a single income-tax return utilizing pass-through taxation.

The company will start off in the black, thanks to an original $50,000 investment ($20,000 savings and a $30,000 Small Business Administration loan payable in 15 years or sooner), and will require no additional financing. The Garcia's will not have to rely on the fledging business for income, since they will use income from Gloria Garcia's freelance consulting jobs to pay personal expenses. The couple has carefully studied the competitive scenario and has already targeted their niche market, much of which is either being overlooked or underserviced by the primary two competing vending operations. Their start-up operating expenses are also estimated to be low because they will store vending products in their home's climate-controlled garage and pay cash for a used cargo van to be used as the company's primary service vehicle.

Snack Break Vending will find its own unique target market due to its focus on healthy snacks and environmentally friendly packaging (drink vendors will only use fully recyclable aluminum cans and avoid plastic bottles). The company's snack vendors will include 25 percent healthy and low-fat snacks and proudly bear a green sticker indicating the company's focus on nutritional products. Snack Break Vending's cold drink machines will include at least one or two fruit juice-based beverages, depending on the vendor size and location, and also bear the green stickers. The environmental focus will be the company's primary marketing tool and the green sticker image will be utilized in all collateral marketing materials, such as business cards, brochures, company stationary, and the planned Web site.

The couple plans a two-pronged marketing campaign to win new vendor locations. In addition to running the home office, Gloria Garcia will implement mass mailing and e-mail campaigns, to be followed up by telemarketing efforts to win personal site visits. Rolando Garcia will do location cold calling, servicing the existing vending routes, and pay site visits for the appointments made by Gloria Garcia.

The Garcias do not plan on needing any additional capital for the first three years because they will be re-investing all of Snack Break Vending proceeds back into the business to purchase new vendors and pay for marketing efforts. After that time period, they will decide if they want to pursue additional capital for financing new growth objectives.

Business Overview

Snack Break Vending is a partnership between the husband and wife team of Rolando and Gloria Garcia based in southeast San Antonio, Texas. Snack Break Vending is a start-up company founded by the pair to provide vending machines and products to an underserved segment of southern Bexar County, the small to mid-sized companies with fewer than 100 employees. The company will also focus on a number of hotel, restaurant, and retail locations located along the I-410 loop of south San Antonio. Snack Break Vending will use a variety of good quality, used tabletop, and free-standing vendors to sell name-brand snacks, cold drinks, and gourmet coffee beverages, as well as concentrating on healthier snack alternatives. The larger vendors will incorporate bill changers for the convenience of the customers. Vending products will be purchased through a variety of outlets, including local soft drink and snack distributors, online companies (primarily for specialty products and bulk buying), and BJ's Wholesale Club, where the couple is a member. During the first six months to a year after start-up, the Garcias will store the merchandise in their garage, which has been climate-controlled, to protect the freshness of the stored merchandise. A larger warehouse will be rented in the future when deemed necessary. They have carefully studied the vending landscape in their area, particularly in southern Bexar County, which is home to a number of smaller companies that do not have the customer value demanded by larger vending operators. The couple's products will do well in their targeted companies because they will have the same price point as the larger vending operators and will guarantee the quality of their products with a no-questions-asked refund policy. The Garcias also have national trends on their side. According to the "2008 State of the Vending Industry Report" released by *Automatic Merchandiser Magazine*, the current vending environment favors the smallest and largest vending operators over mid-size companies.

State of the Industry

The vending sector in the United States is a $22 billion industry. According to figures released recently by Automatic Merchandiser Magazine in its "2008 State of the Vending Industry Report," the industry, like the rest of the food-service sector, is suffering in the present economic downturn. Although revenue growth was dismal across the sector, the vending industry maintained its revenue growth better than other areas of the food-service sector. Although many operators are being squeezed between the high cost of gasoline and the inability to raise prices sufficiently to cover the increased overhead, operators are finding increased sales in the nutritional snack and canned beverage sectors. The former is catching on with the general population after being mandated in schools by the federal government, while the latter is an outgrowth of the environmental movement and aversion to the plastic soda bottles that grew in popularity in the 1990s. Operators are able to see more profit in the canned beverage line because competitors, such as convenience stores, focus more on the 12- and 16-ounce bottle market.

According to the report, more than 36 percent of vending operators focused on manufacturing establishments, which is a declining segment, and the industry as a whole has been slow to adapt to the nation's more prevalent service economy, such as office buildings, retail establishments, and others. Much of the industry's growth in recent years has been through acquisitions of competing vending operations and food and equipment manufacturers.

The industry has several new tools to help position it more solidly in the new millennium, such as vendor-equipped credit and debit card readers, bill recycling, and telemetry, also referred to as remote machine monitoring. The high cost of the new technology, however, is causing pause among all but the largest operators due to economic downturn and a steadily shrinking customer base.

The smallest operators have the advantage of lower overhead to help them compete in today's challenging vending market.

Competitive Analysis and Market Strategies

There are several existing competing vendors in the San Antonio market, including ABC Vending, All Service & Vending, Ben's Vending Service, Full Service Vending, McLiff Vending & Office Coffee Services, San Antonio Snacks, and Vending and Thoene Sales Co. Inc. Of these, ABC and All Service & Vending will be the primary competitors, with the former focusing on smaller locations and the latter located within the company's proposed service area.

Snack Break Vending will differentiate itself from other local operators by touting the company's green focus: healthier snack alternatives and environmentally friendly aluminum-canned drinks instead of hard-to-recycle plastic bottles. The company will concentrate on hotels and motels, small businesses, and retail establishments located within a five-mile radius of I-410 and preferably without a convenience store within easy walking distance. To compete against ABC Vending, Snack Break Vending will stay away from the areas where ABC is known to concentrate — and promote the fact that the Snack Break Vending home base is located within the service area and can offer a quicker response time to product and machine outages. Snack Break Vending will have the advantage over All Service & Vending because the company does not offer honor boxes. The startup will go head-to-head with firms in other locations and be able to offer either higher commission or undercut prices due to its lower overhead.

The company's snack vendors will stock a minimum of 25 percent in healthy snack options and will promote that fact on bright green stickers on each snack vendor. All particular location requests will be honored if feasible and profitable.

Although the company will be competing against the soft drink bottlers' own machines, Snack Break Vending will gain a competitive edge by focusing on the environmentally friendly benefits of highly recyclable aluminum and provide only canned drinks in its vendors, which are also more profitable. The company's canned cold drink vendors will be clearly marked with green environmentally friendly stickers to grab the attention of the public. The company will provide bottler-leased machines in higher traffic locations, or for those that request plastic bottled drinks.

Rolando Garcia will be the primary locator, making cold calls to business and commercial establishments while servicing existing accounts. Gloria Garcia will also help by mailing out brochures and query letters to companies a week or two before Rolando pays a personal visit. The company also plans to promptly launch a Web site to further its marketing efforts.

Operations Plan

Rolando Garcia will be the primary route service person, as well as the public marketing face to the company. Gloria Garcia will man the home office, doing cold-calling and mass mailings to find new vendor locations. She will be responsible for putting the information gleaned from Rolando's route cards into the company's computer system for processing, as well as taking care of all product ordering. Gloria will use the Vending Essentials software program by Software Essentials, Inc. to help manage the company's inventory. She will count and package the cash proceeds, make bank deposits, and field telephone calls from interested location managers.

Rolando will take care of all minor vending repairs, and has already taken apart a used vendor and studied its inner workings before putting it back together in working order. He will also take a more advanced course offered remotely by the National Automatic Merchandising Association. For refrigeration issues, he will contract a family member in the refrigeration and air conditioning business. Snack Break Vending will also keep both a used working snack and drink vendor in the warehouse at all times for use as emergency backup or for harvesting replacement parts quickly.

Management

Rolando and Gloria Garcia are well-equipped to take on the challenge of a family partnership business. Rolando has a background as both a route driver for San Antonio-area beverage bottlers and a route salesman for a major snack food company. His familiarity with vending machines and his experience dealing with the public in a sales capacity makes him ideally suitable for servicing a vending route and finding new locations.

Gloria Garcia boasts a degree in marketing and experience working for various San Antonio non-profit agencies, as well as serving as the office manager for a local medical supplies firm. In addition to her excellent telephone skills, she has inventory management experience and she kept most of the books for the medical firm.

Company Finances

The Garcias are bringing to the table $20,000 of their own funds for start-up operations, as well as a $30,000 Small Business Minority Loan to be paid back in 15 years, if not sooner. Most of the funds will be used to buy start-up vending equipment and merchandise, as well as purchase a used delivery van for route sales. The Garcias will not draw a salary, but will live off Gloria Garcia's earnings as a freelance non-profit consultant and grant writer. Any profit on the business will be plowed back into the company the first year or two of the business.

Income Statement: Snack Break Vending Company

2011 (First 12 months of operations)

	Jan	Feb	mar	apr	may	Jun
sales revenue	$3,820	$4,763	$5,620	$6,535	$6,938	$7,290
Cost of goods sold	($1,320)	($1,683)	($2,008)	($2,360)	($2,508)	($2,640)
Gross profit	**$2,500**	**$3,080**	**$3,612**	**$4,175**	**$4,430**	**$4,650**
operating expenses	($500)	($530)	($570)	($600)	($630)	($650)
Income before taxes	**$2,000**	**$2,550**	**$3,042**	**$3,575**	**$3,800**	**$4,000**
Taxes (10%)	($200)	($255)	($304.20)	($357.50)	($380)	($400)
net income	$1,800	$2,295	$2,737.80	$3,217.50	$3,420	$3,600

	Jul	aug	Sept	oct	nov	dec
sales revenue	$7,813	$8,170	$8,429	$8,777	$9,035	$9,538
Cost of goods sold	($2,838)	($2,970)	($3,069)	($3,207)	($3,300)	($3,498)
Gross profit	**$4,975**	**$5,200**	**$5,360**	**$5,570**	**$5,735**	**$6,040**
operating expenses	($675)	($700)	($710)	($720)	($735)	($740)
Income before taxes	**$4,300**	**$4,500**	**$4,650**	**$4,850**	**$5,000**	**$5,300**
Taxes (10%)	($430)	($450)	($465)	($485)	($500)	($530)
net income	$3,870	$4,050	$4,185	$4,365	$4,500	$4,770

2012 Total	
sales revenue	$115,775
Cost of goods sold	($42,900)
Gross profit	$72,875
operating expenses	($7,875)
Income before taxes	$65,000
Taxes (10%)	($6,500)
net income	$58,500

2013 Total	
sales revenue	$157,700
Cost of goods sold	($59,400)
Gross profit	$98,300
operating expenses	($8,300)
Income before taxes	$90,000
Taxes (10%)	($9,000)
net income	$81,000

Balance sheet: Snack Break Vending Company

	2011	2012	2013
current assets			
Cash on hand	$903	$1,200	$2,500
Inventory	$4,000	$4,800	$9,000
Total current assets	$4,903	$6,000	$11,500
Fixed assets			
Machinery	$19,800	$23,000	$22,500
Vehicles	$10,000	$8,000	$6,000
office equipment	$8,000	$6,400	$4,800
accumulated depreciation	($7,560)	($7,480)	($6,660)
Total fixed assets	$30,240	$29,920	$26,640
Total assets	$35,143	$35,920	$38,140
current liabilities			
accounts payable	$3,460	$3,990	$4,170
Taxes payable	$1,258	$1,380	$3,345
Credit cards	$425	$550	$625
Total current liabilities	$5,143	$5,920	$8,140
long-term liabilities			
sba loan	$30,000	$30,000	$30,000
service vehicle loan	$0	$0	$0
Total long-term liabilities	$30,000	$30,000	$30,000
Total liabilities	$35,143	$35,920	$38,140
Stockholder's equity			
Common stock	$0	$0	$0
Total liabilities and stockholder's equity	$35,143	$35,920	$38,140

	2011	2012	2013
net cash from operations			
Cash received	$47,567	$65,000	$90,000
Cash paid for inventory	($31,401)	($42,900)	($59,400)
Cash paid for operations	($7,760)	($7,975)	($8,300)
Taxes paid	($1,258)	($1,380)	($3,345)
net cash from investments			
additions to equipment or plant	$0	($2,000)	($1,300)
net cash from financing			
Reductions of long-term loans	($2,160)	($2,160)	($2,160)
net increase or (decrease) in cash	**$4,988**	**$8,585**	**$15,495**

Summary

Snack Break Vending has great potential for immediate success and future expansion in the south San Antonio vending sector, due to the Garcias' ample market study and assessment and the procurement of sufficient capital to launch the new business without a lot of overhead or debt on the books. By focusing their marketing efforts on healthy and nutritious snacks and environmentally friendly cold-drink packaging, the couple will find the firm's perfect marketing niche, catering both to the environment- and diet-conscious sectors of the public. Their ability to sow all of the company's proceeds back into the business the first few years for purchasing equipment and winning new locations will enable the company to prosper and grow without undue restrictions.

APPENDIX B

Vending and Business Resources

Amusement Machines

Magic Play — **www.magicplay.us**

Impulse Industries — **www.impulseamusements.com**

Bill and Coin Receptor Repair

Vendor's Repair Service, Inc. — **www.vendorsrepair.com**

Bulk-Vending Machine Manufacturers

Actionmatic, Ltd. — **www.actionmatic.com**

Oak Manufacturing Company, Inc. — **www.oakmfg.com**

OK Manufacturing — **www.okmfg.net**

Bulk Vendors and Products

A&A Global Industries, Inc. — **www.aaglobalind.com**

Actionmatic, Ltd. — **www.actionmatic.com**

Allstar Vending — **www.allstarvending.com**

Brand Imports, LLC — **www.brandvendingproducts.com**

Big Apple Vending & Supply Corporation —
www.bigapplevending.com

Candymachines.com — **www.candymachines.com**

Cutting Edge TNT — **www.ceistickers.com**

Gumball Machine Warehouse — **www.gumball-machine.com**

TNT-Amusements Vending — **www.tntamusements.net**

Business Mentoring

SCORE — **www.score.org**

Business Incubators

The National Business Incubation Association
20 East Circle Dr. No. 37198
Athens, OH 45701-3751
Phone: 740-593-4331
Fax: 740-593-1996
www.nbia.org

Business Startup Advice

U.S. Small Business Administration — **www.sba.gov**

StartupNation, LLC — **www.startupnation.com**

Business Nation — **www.businessnation.com**

Entrepreneur Media, Inc. — **www.entrepreneur.com**

HowtoStartup.com — **www.howtostartup.com**

DevStart Inc. — **www.businessownersideacafe.com**

Coin and Currency Counters

Factory-Express, Inc. — **www.factory-express.com**

Heavenly Office — **www.heavenlyoffice.com/money1.htm**

Currency Counter Store — **www.currencycounterstore.com**

Cash Register Distributors Warehouse — **www.crdw.com/store**

Computers and Peripherals

TigerDirect — **www.tigerdirect.com**

Gateway — **www.gateway.com**

Dell — **www.dell.com**

Shopzilla, Inc. — **www.bizrate.com/laptopcomputers/**

Computer Desks and Other Office Equipment and Supplies

Office Depot, Inc. — **www.officedepot.com**

Staples — **www.staples.com**

Quill Lincolnshire, Inc. — **www.quillcorp.com**

Credit Reporting Agencies

Equifax
P.O. Box 740241
Atlanta, GA 30374
Toll-free: 888-202-4025
www.equifax.com

Experian
475 Anton Blvd.
Costa Mesa, CA 92626
Phone: 714-830-7000
www.experian.com

TransUnion
2 Baldwin Place
P.O. Box 2000
Chester, PA 19022
Toll-free: 800-888-4213
www.transunion.com

Employee Handbook Templates and Advice

Human Resources & Information Technology, Inc. —
www.hrit.com

CertifiedEmployeeHandbook.com —
www.certifiedemployeehandbook.com

Your Employee Handbook —
http://youremployeehandbook.com

Business Know-How/Employee Handbook Template —
www.businessknowhow.net/employeehandbook.asp

Employee Health and Safety Resources

Occupational Safety and Health Administration (OSHA)
200 Constitution Ave. NW
Washington, DC 20210
www.osha.gov

Online training tool for OSHA safety requirements —
www.free-training.com/osha/Soshamenu.htm

John Burton's Workers' Compensation Resources —
www.workerscompresources.com

Honor Snack Tray Companies

Westgate Systems, Inc.
Phone: 715-832-6013
www.westgatesystemsinc.com

Kiddie Rides

Theisen Vending Company
2335 Nevada Ave. N
Golden Valley, MN 55427
Toll-free: 800-633-3436
Phone: 612-827-5588
Fax: 612-827-7543
www.theisenvending.com

Kosher Vendors and Products

Kosher Vending Industries
898 Washington St.
Peekskill, NY 10566
Phone: 845-268-1818

Sheridan Systems
Phone: 716-873-7003
www.sheridansystems.com

Locating Services

Kick Start Locations
3742 Whidbey Way.
Naples, FL 34119
www.kickstartlocations.com

Name Administration Inc.
Phone: 877-850-2934
www.vendorlocators.com

Advanced Placement Services
369 Highway 315
Fortson, GA 31808
Phone: 1-866-561-6021
www.vendingplacement.com

A1 Best Locators
18034 Ventura Blvd. No. 493
Encino, CA 91316
Phone: 800-746-7702
www.a1bestlocators.com

Business Beanstalk Vending Locator
253 Virginia Ave.
San Mateo, CA 94402
Phone: 800-472-3637
Fax: 650-249-0107
www.myvendinglocator.com

Carlin Cotton 1, LLC
302 West Howry Ave.
DeLand, Florida 32721
Phone: 386-847-6171
www.candyvendinglocating.com

Natural and Organic Vendors and Products

Yo-Naturals Incorporated
4380 La Jolla Village Dr. No. 230
San Diego, CA 92122
Phone: 858-794-9955
Phone: 858-794-9959
www.yonaturals.com

Payroll Tax Issues

Real Business Solutions – Payroll Mate
PO Box 1010
Orland Park, IL USA 60462
www.realtaxtools.com

Intuit QuickBooks — **www.quickbooks.intuit.com**

Service Vehicles

Marshal's Motors, The Aluminum Stepvan Resource
1027 Washington St.
Decatur, IN 46733
Phone: 260-724-4414
Fax: 260-301-0005
www.stepvans.com

Trucker.com — **www.trucker.com**

TruckFinders, Inc.
Phone: 940-464-2200
Fax: 940-240-0009
www.truckfindersinc.com

Sandhills Publishing Company – Truck Paper
P.O. Box 85010
Lincoln, NE 68501-5673
Phone: 800-247-4868
Fax: 402-479-2134
www.truckpaper.com

Trade Magazines

American Automatic Merchandiser
1233 Janesville Ave.
Fort Atkinson, WI 53538-0803
Phone: 800-547-7377
Fax: 920-328-9029
www.automaticmerchandiser.com

RePlay Magazine (entertainment machine news only)
18757 Burbank Blvd. #105
Tarzana, CA 91356
Phone: 818-776-2880
Fax: 818-776-2888
www.replaymag.com

Vending Times
55 Maple Ave. Suite 102
Rockville Centre, NY 11570
Phone: 516-442-1850

Fax: 516-442-1849
www.vendingtimes.com

Vending Business Software Programs

Vending Essentials
Toll-free: 800-971-0023
www.softessentials.com

VendMax
1327 Border Street
Winnipeg, Manitoba R3H 0N1
Toll-free: 800-661-1832
Phone: 204-697-5900
Fax: 204-694-8700
www.vendmax.com

Validata Computer & Research Corporation
428 S. Perry St.
Montgomery, AL 36104
Phone: 334-834-2324
Fax: 334-262-5648
For RouteSail Millennia and other vending software **www.validata.
    com/products.htm**

Vending Industry Advice and Telephone Consultations

Vending Rules — **www.vendingrules.com**

My Vending Secret — **www.myvendingsecret.com**

Vending Industry Information

The Vending Authority — **www.vendingauthority.com**

Vendline — **www.vendline.com**

Vintage Vending — **www.vintagevending.com**

Vending Machines (New and Used)

Breaktime Vending, Inc.
60 Long Lake
Carriere, MS 39426
Phone: 601-749-8424 ext. 11
Fax: 601-749-8425
www.usedvending.com

The Wittern Group
8040 University Blvd.
Des Moines, IA 50325
Phone: 515-274-3641
Toll-free: 866-657-7549
Fax: 515-271-8530
www.wittern.com

Vending Machines Unlimited
432 S. Washington Ave. #1602
Royal Oak, MI 48067
Toll-free: 800-380-6312
www.vendingmachinesunlimited.com

Vendweb.com
1735 Dameron Rd.
Bessemer City, NC 28016
Phone: 704-802-4394
Fax: 704-802-4395
www.vendweb.com

Vendors Equipment Inc.
1172 North Main Street
P.O. Box 4832
Waterbury, CT 06704
Phone: 203-574-5983
Fax: 203-574-0405
www.vendorsequipment.com

Vending On Demand
8411 Nieman Rd
Lenexa, KS 66214
Toll-free: 877-983-6346
Phone: 913-299-2444
Fax: 913-273-0505
www.vendingondemand.com

Vendors Exchange International, Inc.
8700 Brookpark Road
Cleveland, OH 44129
Phone: 216-432-1800
Toll Free: 800-321-2311
www.veii.com

VE South L.C.
4800 N.W. 15th Ave., Suite B
Fort Lauderdale, FL 33309
Phone: 954-491-7300
Toll-free: 888-837-6884
Fax: 954-491-7301
www.vesouth.com

Vending Massage Chairs

Massage Manufacturers Direct, Inc.
2050 Concourse Dr. #50
San Jose, CA 95131
Toll-free: 1-888-487-3362
Fax: 408-955-0211
www.dollar-massage.com

The Back Rubber, Inc.
1170-6 Lincoln Ave
Holbrook, NY 11741
Toll-free: 866-919-8363
Phone: 631-750-5988
Fax: 631-389-2530
www.thebackrubber.com

Vending Trade Organizations and Related Web Sites

Vending Yellow Pages — www.vendingconnection.com

National Automatic Merchandisers Association
20 N. Wacker Drive, Suite 3500
Chicago, IL 60606
Phone: 312-346-0370
www.vending.org

The National Bulk Vendors Association
7782 E. Greenway Road, Suite 2
Scottsdale, AZ 85256-1706
Phone: 480-302-5998
Fax: 480-302-5108
www.nbva.org

Web Site Design and Hosting

Affordable Web Design and E-Commerce, Inc. —
   www.affordablewebdesign.com

Expedite Media Group
2 South Broadway – 2nd floor

Aurora, IL 60505
Phone: 630-897-6448
Fax: 630-897-6895
www.expeditemg.com

Homestead Technologies, Inc. — **www.homestead.com**

Network Solutions, LLC — **www.networksolutions.com**

Glossary of Vending Terms

Balance sheet: One of the three parts of a pro forma financial statement; this is an close-up of a company's assets, liabilities, and equity during a specific time period.

Bill changer: A small box attached to a mechanical vending machine or freestanding larger unit, whose sole purpose is to receive paper currency and dispense change for vending machines.

Bill receptors or acceptors: The slot on a vending machine that is able to read and accept currency payments, usually $1 bills, but occasionally larger denominations depending on the kind of vendor.

Bins, columns, or spirals: The separate vending spaces of a vending machine to which rows of specific products or items are assigned. Most newer snack vendors utilize spirals that twist to dispense the product. The term "column" is primarily used for cold-drink vendors.

Bottler-serviced machines or vendors: Beverage machines that are serviced by a soft drink or beverage-bottling company, and whose original location agreement is arranged by a vending operator who receives a regular commission check.

Box truck: A vehicle occasionally used by vending operators that is similar to many of the larger self-moving trucks, which are basically a big box attached to a truck chassis behind the cab. These vehicles frequently include an incorporated lift at the rear, which is ideal for raising and lowering stacks of cold drinks and vending machines.

Bulk operator: A vending company or route person who services vending machines that dispense a portion-controlled amount of gumballs, candies, or nuts, as well as stickers or small toys in plastic eggs.

Bulk vending: The sale of snacks, candies, or non-food items in bulk vendors designed to dispense a measured or weighed portion of food or a packaged toy, stickers, or other merchandise.

Business plan: A comprehensive document that will form the framework for a business. A good plan includes several components, including a cover page, executive summary, business overview, state of the industry, competitive analysis and marketing strategies, operations plan, management overview, and company finances.

Cash-and-carry: The informal vending term used to describe wholesale club-like stores, which are frequently used as a product source for smaller vending operators. The name is derived from the fact that business owners can purchase items in bulk, usually at a discount, but must pay cash or with another similar form of payment rather than be invoiced at 30 days net, as is common with most product distributors. Vendors who produce a sales tax identification number can also purchase products without having to pay sales tax.

Cash-flow statement: One of the three parts of a pro forma financial statement; this document highlights a company's total cash received and spent through the normal operation of conducting business.

Charity sponsorship: An agreement with a local or national non-profit organization, frequently used by bulk candy and snack vending operators to pay a small percentage (usually 10 percent or less) to the organization for the use of logos, images, and stickers on the vendors. Operators frequently use the sponsorships as a selling point for winning placement approval at locations.

Coin mechanism: The mechanical or electronic part of a vending machine that counts the coins inserted and dispenses change after a selection is made.

Cold calling: The act of paying a personal visit to the respective managers of potential vendor locations, none of whom have any advance notice of your visit, to try and create interest in your vending or other business. Also, the act of telephoning the same people without their having any prior knowledge of your business or the purpose of your call.

Commission: A percentage of gross sales frequently paid to locations for the right to place a vendor or vendors on the property. These can range from 10 to 30 percent or higher, depending on the individual location agreement.

Cup mechanism: The part of a beverage machine that dispenses a plastic or Styrofoam cup, into which a measured amount of soft drink, coffee, hot chocolate, or other beverage is dispensed.

Cycle: The set amount of time required for a particular vendor to dispense a product.

Distributor: A company that usually serves as the middleman between the customer and the manufacturer to reach a broader section of the market. Distributors frequently carry a variety of products made by several different manufacturers.

Drum: The rotating horizontal sleeves of a product vendor.

Employee handbook: The manual given to all company employees that outlines important company procedures and policies. These usually cover everything from sexual harassment, theft, employee vacation, and holiday time.

FICA: The acronym for the Federal Insurance Contributions Act, which also stands for the combined federal taxes known as Medicare and social security.

Free vend: A specific period of time during which a vendor is set to dispense its products without charge. Usually done as a perk or reward for a good location during a business meeting or other event.

Full-line vending: The incorporation of frozen and refrigerated foods to the snack and soda line.

Honor system vending: A system of snack trays and drink refrigerators whose products are sold on the "honor system;" in other words, people place their own money for the products in a cash box located directly on the tray.

Income statement: One of the three parts of the pro forma financial statements; the income analysis details income and expenses for a specific time period, usually a month, quarter, or year.

Limited liability company: A newer business structure available in most states that functions as a hybrid between incorporation and a sole proprietorship.

Locating company: A business whose primary mission is to provide vendor-locating services to vending business owners. Such companies frequently contract their work out to outside locators who have no other ties to the company in question. Frequently used by biz-op promoters to provide locations in bulk.

Location manager: The person with whom a vending operator deals and who has the authority to accept vendors and vending agreements and sign a contract, if necessary. Also, the representative of a large vending operation who is responsible for overseeing the vending operations of a particular location.

Location: A particular business, company, building, or other structure where a vending operator has vending machines.

Long-term debt: The amount of money owed to outside lending institutions for loans and other debts, usually payable in terms of longer than one year.

Manufacturer: A company that fabricates equipment, such as vending machines, or products like food or beverage items, to stock in vendors. Most manufacturers market their products through distributors, although some will send their items directly to business owners and operators.

Marginal locations: Vending locations that are not considered profitable because of the limited amount of potential customer traffic. Such locations are occasionally subsidized by the resident company or companies so the operator can make a profit. These are sometimes used by vending companies to fill up gaps in service route scheduling.

Marketing: The act of choosing the right products, promotions and pricing for your area of distribution. Marketing efforts can include cold calling, telemarketing, and mass mailings to create awareness for your business. Marketing and public relations frequently work hand-in-hand.

Meter: A small device attached to a vending machine to count and record the amount of vending cycles.

Mission statement: This is the core principal around which any successful business is built. Ranging from a couple of sentences to a few paragraphs, your company's mission statement should include your firm's reason for existence, who it serves, where it operates, what it sells, and what makes your product or service unique.

NAMA: The acronym for the National Automatic Merchandising Association, the largest trade organization servicing the vending and contract food-service industries.

Niche vending: Vending a specific product or products to a particularly focused segment of the population that not many other vendors are catering to.

OCS: The acronym for Office Coffee System, which is a service frequently supplied by full-line operators as an added benefit to their best clients. Not considered very profitable, OCS is frequently used as a tool to win a location's complete vending service business.

Operating expenses: The monthly reoccurring expenses that a company must satisfy, which include rent and utilities, service vehicles and fuel, employee salaries, and other costs.

Par level: The minimum amount of a particular item in stock, signifying that a reorder is essential to maintain proper inventory flow.

Par sheet: A list of products by name, par level (see above) amount currently in inventory, the amount to be ordered immediately to bring the item above par, and the name of the distributor or supplier, among other things.

Partnership: A business model by which two or more equal partners decide to do business together as one company, but file their income taxes separately under the pass-through type of system, by which they list their predetermined percentage of the business's proceeds as income directly onto the IRS Form 1040. Either partner can make decisions that affect the business and both partners will be bound by them.

Limited liability partnership (LLP): Similar to a limited partnership, except that all partners are immune from personal liability. Many states limit these to lawyers, accountants, and other professionals susceptible to lawsuits.

Limited partnership: A partnership of unequal partners: One has decision-making authority and the other, the limited partner, is primarily the business backer, or silent partner. The latter is also shielded from personal liability.

Pass-through taxation: The form by which the owner of a sole proprietorship or the members of a partnership pay their taxes by directly listing the company's proceeds on IRS Form 1040 as income. In the case of one or more partners, the partners would list their exact percentage of the company's revenue as income on Form 1040.

Planogram: A diagram of a specific vending machine to show which products are to be stocked on specific spirals, bins, or columns.

Product markup: The price set for the wholesale or retail cost of an item that will earn the business a profit after the cost of purchasing the product and marketing it are discounted.

Profit: The amount of revenue left over to a business after the cost of products, labor, distribution, and infrastructure are taken into account.

Proposal: A written description of exactly what a vending company will provide for a particular location and describes the payment of commissions or charity sponsorships, if utilized.

Public relations: The best face of a company put forth through the marketing efforts of the owners or operators. This includes membership in local business and civic organizations, media contacts with press releases announcing new product launches, or community participation by the company and in other outreaches done in the name of the business. The ultimate goal of public relations is to bring cost-free publicity to the company and its offerings.

Remote monitoring: See telemetry.

Route cards or reports: Index or larger-size note cards used to record all pertinent information about the particular servicing of a location's vendors, such as the date, vendor number(s), amount of money collected, number of snacks and beverages sold, refund amounts disbursed, and quantity of products wasted.

Route driver: The individual assigned to a particular vending route.

Route: A particular series of vending locations that is located relatively in the same area or encompasses the same type of vending items, which are usually serviced on the same day of the week or month on a regular basis.

Self-employment taxes: The taxes paid, usually quarterly, by sole proprietors and members of partnerships. These include income taxes and 100 percent of FICA taxes (social security and Medicare).

Service vehicle: Any type of vehicle used to carry merchandise to restock vendors on a vending route. This can be a car, van, pickup truck, step-van, box truck, or other type of vehicle pressed into service.

Servicing: The act of replenishing the stock of a vendor, removing the proceeds from the previous week or month of sales and wiping down the exterior services. Vendors are also verified to be operating properly during servicing and repairs done on site, if possible.

Shrinkage: The loss of product to theft or non-payment; a term frequently used in the honor box vending sector. A certain amount of shrinkage is frequently considered acceptable among honor box vendors since the product markup is usually high enough to offset a certain percentage of losses.

Slave machine: A vendor that does not have its own computer or selection buttons and must be attached to another machine where the selections are made.

Snack and soda vending: The most popular form of vending that includes snack machine vendors, which sell chips, candies, nuts, and other products, along with cold drink machines.

Sole proprietorship: A vending or any other kind of business run by only one person who pays his or her income taxes in the pass-through form of taxation.

Spiral: The most common form of modern vending machines to vend their products. Individual bags of snack items are hung on spirals, which twist or turn the exact amount of distance during the vend for the item to fall into the vend area below.

Step van: A vehicle frequently used by vending operators, which is similar to the ones used by the United Parcel Service and other delivery companies. The interior is tall enough in which to stand up, and the interior aisle makes stocking and filling orders easier compared to a standard delivery van.

Target marketing: The act of focusing a company's primary marketing strategy toward the goal of reaching a defined, specific subset of the population that is most likely to buy the products in question.

Telemetry: Commonly referred to as remote monitoring, this is a form of electronic communication by which an automatic vending device communicates product information to a central computer or e-mail address so the operator or location manager knows that a product is out or a vendor is malfunctioning.

Vend: The vending machine cycle during which the purchase and delivery of a single item is completed.

Vending location contract: A legal document by which a location manager agrees to the placement of a vendor on the premises by a vending operator, as well as other stipulations, such as the minimum length of time or commission amount.

Vending operator: A person who owns, stocks, and services vending machines that sell snacks, drinks, small toys, or other merchandise.

Vendor: A common name used for any type of vending machine that sells a product in exchange for inserting coins, currency, or magnetic strip cards; frequently used to describe a vending machine operator or the owner of a vending business.

Bibliography

Breaktime Vending (**www.usedvending.com**)

Bob's Vending Repair Service (**www.bvrsales.com**)

Jed, Emily. "Kosher Vending Industries Meets Growing Away-From-Home Demand," *Vending Times*, July 2008.

King, Paul, "Technology Gap: Cost Keep Latest Vending Operations Out of Reach for Most Vending Operators," Nation's Restaurant News, April 2004.

Kosher Vending (**www.koshervendingindustries.com**)

Lesonsky, Rieva, *Start Your Own Business, 4th Edition*, Entrepreneur Press, 2007.

Maras, Elliot, "2008 State of the Vending Industry Report," *Automatic Merchandiser*, 2008.

Mintzer, Richard, *Start Your Own Vending Business: Your Step-by-Step Guide to Success*, Entrepreneur Press, 2007.

My Vending Uncle (**www.my-vending-uncle.com**)

National Automatic Merchandising Association
(**www.vending.org**)

Pakroo, Peri, *The Small Business Start-Up Kit: A Step-by-Step Legal Guide, 5th Edition*, NOLO, 2008.

Paulson, Ed, *The Complete Idiot's Guide to Starting Your Own Business, 5th Edition*, Alpha, 2007.

Talent, Ronnie, *The Vending Jackpot: How to Build and Manage Your Own Profitable Vending Business*, TGI Publishing, 2001.

Vending Connection (**www.vendingconnection.com**)

Vending Rules (**www.vendingrules.com**)

Way, Bill, *Vending Success Secrets: How Anyone Can Grow Rich in America's Best Cash Business! 3rd Edition*, Freedom Tech Press, 2001.

Woodbine, Steven, *Vending Machine Fundamentals: How To Build Your Own Route*, Pratzen Publishing, 2007.

Yo-Naturals (**www.yonaturals.com**)

Author Biographies

D onald Rodrigue is a seasoned reporter, writer, and editor who has worked in every aspect of journalism, from beat reporting to news and travel writing to corporate communications. After earning a degree in journalism from the University of Southern Mississippi in 1993, he began his career in the mid-1990s as a reporter for a small daily newspaper in Picayune, Mississippi, just north of New Orleans. From August 1996 to December 1997, he lived in Costa Rica, where he picked up the Spanish language and honed his travel writing skills. Upon his return to the United States, he eventually ended up in Miami. There, for almost nine years, he worked as an associate editor for HCP/ Aboard, a custom-publishing division of the *Miami Herald* and the McClatchy Co. During that time, he perfected his skills as a travel writer, traveling up and down the Western Hemisphere from San Francisco to Peru documenting his experiences. One of the last travel pieces he wrote for the company on Western culture and the rodeo in Houston earned him a prestigious Magnum Opus Award in 2008. Since leaving the company to relocate to Port St. Lucie, Florida, Rodrigue has been covering community news on the Treasure Coast and freelance writing for a variety of publications. He also drew on his own business experience for his latest endeavor in authoring *How to Open & Operate a Financially Successful Vending Business*. From 1988 to 1995, he worked as the sole proprietor of his own business, Rodrigue's Wholesale Company, buying and selling merchandise and running more than a dozen sales routes through Alabama, Louisiana, and Mississippi.

Donna M. Murphy is an editorial specialist who is proficient in technical and business communications. She is a published author who has written, edited, and designed extensive collateral and key solutions products for print and the Web. Training manuals, operating procedures, business publications, and content quality assurance encompass a large portion of her assignments. She provides editorial and publication design services for industries, such as information technology, entrepreneurial and business, and publishing and communications. Prior to establishing her editorial and design company, Murphy worked as a computer systems analyst, Web content editor, technical copywriter, and communications instructor for various clients, including Hewlett-Packard, Motorola, General Electric, Texas Children's Hospital, Shell, and Colorado State University. Murphy is the author of two books: *Organize Your Books In 6 Easy Steps* and *The Woman's Guide to Self-Publishing*. She has also published numerous resource booklets and has been featured in various magazines, business journals, and online communities, including *Real Women Real Issues, Work.Home.You, The Old Schoolhouse Magazine, Bizymoms,* and *BamBiz.*

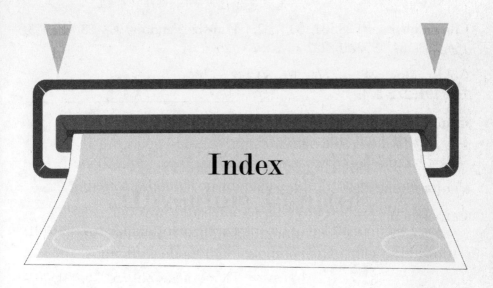

Index